my DOG has HIP DYSPLASIA – but lives life to the full!

www.hubbleandhattie.com

The Hubble & Hattie imprint was launched in 2009 and is named in memory of two very special Westies owned by Veloce's proprietors.

Since the first book, many more have been added to the list, all with the same underlying objective: to be of real benefit to the species they cover, at the same time promoting compassion, understanding and co-operation between all animals (including human ones!)

Hubble & Hattie is the home of a range of books that cover all-things animal, produced to the same high quality of content and presentation as our motoring books, and offering the same great value for money.

More titles from Hubble & Hattie

Animal Grief: How animals mourn each other (Alderton)
Cat Speak (Rauth-Widmann)
Clever dog! Life lessons from the world's most successful animal (O'Meara)
Complete Dog Massage Manual, The – Gentle Dog Care (Robertson)
Dieting with my dog (Frezon)
Dog Cookies (Schöps)
Dog Games – stimulating play to entertain your dog and you (Blenski)
Dog Speak (Blenski)
Emergency First Aid for dogs (Bucksch)
Exercising your puppy: a gentle & natural approach – Gentle Dog Care (Robertson & Pope)
Fun and Games for Cats (Seidl)
Know Your Dog – The guide to a beautiful relationship (Birmelin)
My dog is blind – but lives life to the full! (Horsky)
My dog is deaf – but lives life to the full! (Willms)
My dog has hip dysplasia – but lives life to the full! (Haüsler)
My dog has cruciate ligament injury – but lives life to the full! (Haüsler)
Older Dog, Living with an – Gentle Dog Care (Alderton & Hall)
Smellorama – nose games for dogs (Theby)
Swim to recovery: canine hydrotherapy healing – Gentle Dog Care (Wong)
Waggy Tails & Wheelchairs (Epp)
Walking the dog: motorway walks for drivers & dogs (Rees)
Winston ... the dog who changed my life (Klute)
You and Your Border Terrier – The Essential Guide (Alderton)
You and Your Cockapoo – The Essential Guide (Alderton)

Acknowledgements

We are very grateful to Dr Anke Lotze, who gave us the impetus to write this book, and vet Dr Peter Morlock, who was always there for us with an encouraging word or two.

In particular, we would like to thank all our dogs: Dago, Kalypso, and Argos, and all the others with whom Barbara Friedrich has lived and worked, Dr Kirsten Häusler's dog Nala – gone too soon – who taught us many things, and, of course, her current dogs, Itchy and Dexter.

Whilst the authors and Veloce Publishing Ltd have designed this book to provide up-to-date information regarding the subject matter covered, readers should be aware that medical information is constantly evolving. The information in this book is not intended as a substitute for veterinary medical advice. Readers should consult their veterinary surgeon for specific instructions on the treatment and care of their dog. The authors and Veloce Publishing Ltd shall have neither liability nor responsibility with respect to any loss, damage, or injury caused, or alleged to be caused directly or indirectly, by the information contained within this book.

First published in English in July 2011 by Veloce Publishing Limited, Veloce House, Parkway Farm Business Park, Middle Farm Way, Poundbury, Dorchester, Dorset, DT1 3AR, England. Fax 01305 250479/e-mail info@hubbleandhattie.com/web www.hubbleandhattie.com

ISBN: 978-1-845843-82-3 UPC: 6-36847-04382-7. Original publication © 2011 Kynos Verlag Dr Dieter Fleig GmbH, www.kynos-verlag.de

Readers with ideas for books about animals, or animal-related topics, are invited to write to the editorial director of Veloce Publishing at the above address.

British Library Cataloguing in Publication Data – A catalogue record for this book is available from the British Library. Typesetting, design and page make-up all by Veloce Publishing Ltd on Apple Mac.

Printed in India by Imprint Digital.

9/11 B&T

Contents

Chapter 1

Hip Dysplasia (HD): tips, pain reduction & treatment

When I bought my first puppy, I visited the breeder, saw the mother and the litter, and everything seemed fine. I signed a purchase agreement, the breeder brought the little puppy to me, I paid for him, and immediately fell in love with my new, four-legged friend.

It amazed me how well the puppy got on with my children. I thought about all the things he would need, such as food, a cage, and toys. But not for one moment did I give any thought to illness and disease, or even to heredity. We were lucky, Dago and I: he lived with us for 15 happy, mostly healthy years.

A few years later came our second dog. In the purchase agreement, there was a clause which obliged me to have my dog X-rayed within 12-14 months, and to send the X-rays to the OFA (the Orthopaedic Foundation for Animals) for evaluation.

Why? Because the breeder wanted to ensure that none of her puppies had HD, although both parents were free of HD, and my dog was healthy. My dog would have to be given an anaesthetic to be X-rayed, and I wasn't convinced that this was a good idea.

Today, this clause is a part of many puppy purchase agreements. But even though owners may have paid a certain amount in advance, which is returned to them after the X-ray, a lot fail to get their puppy X-rayed. Many wonder, as I did at the time, whether they should put themselves and their dog through this ordeal ...?

Why all the fuss, then?

And what if, at the end of the procedure, you get bad news? What does it mean if your dog has moderate HD? Or even severe HD? Wouldn't it be better not to know?

Of course, no one can force you to have your dog X-rayed, but dog owners who decide they would rather not know won't be able to deal as quickly with any problems, should they arise, whilst those who

In spite of her HD, Kalypso lived to almost 14 years of age.

are aware early on can prevent and avoid the worst.

So let's look at the concerns and considerations. Okay, to have the tests requires time and money, but the time involved is only a fraction of that you'll spend with your four-legged friend over the next 10-15 years. With regard to the cost, consider this: compared to the amount you will spend on food, vet visits, toys, etc, over the same period of time, the cost of this procedure is peanuts.

Forewarned is forearmed. If you are unaware that your dog is at risk, you could unwittingly cause him harm by over-exercising him and feeding him the wrong diet. By avoiding this, not only will you protect your dog, but also your wallet. Treatment for HD can be very expensive, and prevention is always better than cure, but, apart from any other considerations, you and your dog would miss out on a lot of joy over the time you have together.

Radiation

Modern X-ray equipment uses very low doses of radiation, and the anaesthetic is usually a minimal risk. However, if you later have to treat your dog for HD, this X-ray will give you and your vet a good indication of the severity of the HD, and will show whether or not your dog needs an operation.

What about the stress involved? No dog likes going to the vet, but HD, along with the osteoarthritis which accompanies it, will be painful and severely limit your dog's movement; it also necessitates frequent visits to the vet ...

I thought it would be a good idea to educate myself about HD, and, today, I am happy that I allowed my dog, Kalypso, to be X-rayed and had the results analysed. Over the years that I've had a dog I have seen dogs suffering with HD, and am relieved that we were able to avoid this problem for Kalypso. At the time, the discovery that she was at risk of HD forced me to pay close attention to her nutrition, monitor her weight regularly, and observe strict rules about exercise. Because of this, Kalypso's HD never developed. She died at almost 14 years of age, after her second stroke.

The aim of this book is to inform you about HD. We strongly recommend an examination; once you have the result, you can shape your life with your dog, depending on his health, with preventative action, and relieve your dog's suffering through correct nutrition and exercise. Despite a diagnosis of HD, you can still enjoy many different activities with your dog – but you need to know how to prevent further damage in that case. We very much hope that this will allow you to look forward to many fun-filled years with your four-legged friend!

Chapter 2
The anatomy of HD

What does a hip joint look like?

The thigh bone (also known as the femur) and pelvis are connected by the hip joint. The upper end of the femur is almost spherical; this is called the joint head, or the ball, and it fits neatly into the hip socket, which is curved to ensure the ball is a good fit, without friction.

The hip is a ball and socket joint which allows not only forwards and backwards movement, but also sideways movement. Connective tissue, various ligaments, and muscles surround the joint and hold it together, collectively known as the joint capsule or the articular capsule.

Before birth, bones and joints have cartilage cores. Whilst a puppy, these are soft and malleable, to a degree. As the puppy grows, they gradually become solid, as the body replaces the cartilage in the growth plate with bone; a process known as ossification. Weight-bearing, within reason, helps promote the ossification process.

The ball and socket head are coated with cartilage that is smooth, moist, and elastic.

Think of a door hinge: this will open without a sound if the hinge is lubricated. But if there's no – or inadequate – lubrication, it squeaks and creaks, and may even become stuck.

In order to function properly, the hip joint has to be lubricated. The joint lubricant (synovial fluid) is like the grease (graphite, silicon, etc) in a hinge. Synovial fluid is a clear, slightly viscous bodily fluid, which contains moisture and fat, amongst other things. The body makes this fluid within the joint capsule, thus ensuring smooth, painless movement.

What is HD?

HD stands for 'hip dysplasia.' The medical dictionary defines dysplasia as: 'a malformation or slippage of a tissue or organ.' Therefore, hip dysplasia is a malformation or slippage of the hip joint.

HD also occurs in humans: some

babies even have to wear a brace to ensure that their hips develop properly.

What's wrong, exactly?

With HD, the ball and joint socket don't fit together as they should. This could be because the socket is not curved enough, or the ball is not the right shape in order to fit properly into the socket, either of which will impair joint function.

The normal musculoskeletal system keeps bones and joint capsules in position. But when the connective tissue of the articular capsule is too slack, the joint – despite the support provided by the muscles – is not held in place properly. The muscles are often too weak to support the joint adequately, which further increases instability, and, in turn, aggravates the nerve endings, causing unbearable pain.

Another problem is that the cartilage that coats the ball and socket wears and becomes rough, and is more susceptible to abrasion as a result. In contrast to articular cartilage, there are no blood vessels to feed the bone in order to repair the damaged cartilage, and the synovial fluid alone is not sufficient to regenerate the damaged cartilage.

As a result, the cartilage gradually disappears, leaving bone to rub against bone: this is extremely painful, even if only a very small area is affected. Should this happen, in order to avoid further pain, the dog, understandably, will adjust his style of walking, which causes some muscles to become strained, whilst others are hardly used, resulting in muscle wastage. The joint then becomes even looser and the HD gets worse and worse – a painful, vicious circle.

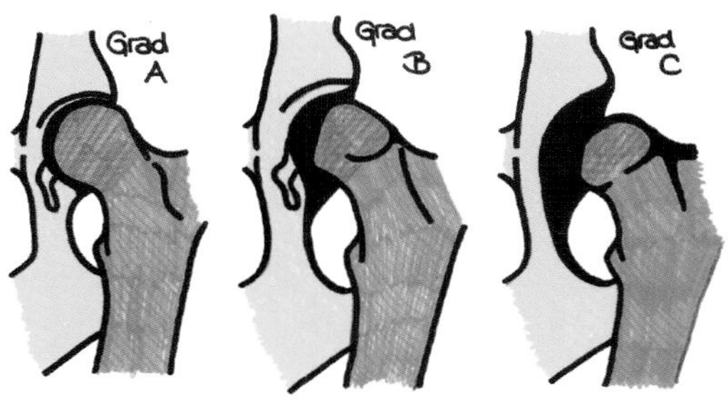

The more serious the HD, the looser the hip joint is in the socket.

What is the cause of HD?

The answer to this is not simple, and scientists are still researching the primary causes of HD. It is thought, however, that several factors can contribute.

Is HD hereditary?

Some dogs inherit a very serious deformation of the joint socket from one, or even both, parents. Such dogs should not be bred, and most breeders are very keen to stamp out HD, though it's not enough to select only HD-free dogs, or dogs with minor malformations, for breeding. Inheritance is a complicated matter, and even HD-free parents may inherit a predisposition to the disease; a certain susceptibility to a disease or abnormality, which means they have a genetic tendency toward the disease, under certain circumstances. Unfortunately, this genetic tendency doesn't show up in an X-ray.

To limit the incidence of HD, a huge amount of data must be collected to assess canine offspring, comparing the information of many dogs, and taking into account all the possible abnormalities, by determining whether the dogs were raised in such a way as to minimise their chances of developing the condition, or in such a way that increased their chances of this.

Remember: this is a tricky subject, but we don't want to become bogged down in the different opinions of every breeder association. For the moment, we will assume that, in addition to genetic predisposition, a dog's nutrition and exercise routine play an important role in bone and muscle formation, and are, therefore, connected to the development of HD. The aim of this book is to guide you on how to minimise the risk of HD for your dog, how to make life easier for him if he has HD, and how to make sure he lives a mostly pain-free life. We also advise about possible treatments, diet, exercise, and specific training.

Sadly, there are instances of dogs with very deformed hips, which mean that a life without suffering is not possible. In these cases, your vet may advise euthanasia.

Why does my dog need an anaesthetic for the X-ray?

In order for the hip joint to be X-rayed, the dog must lie stretched out on his back, with his legs turned slightly inward. No dog would remain in a relaxed state on the X-ray table in this position, not even if you and a couple of helpers were to hold him in position, and nor would a sedative keep him calm. Therefore, a diagnostically conclusive X-ray is only possible under a short-term anaesthetic. It is worth noting that there are several different X-ray procedures.

Why does the X-ray need to be analysed by an expert?

Surely my vet has sufficient knowledge to analyse the X-ray himself?

Your vet certainly will be very knowledgeable, and deserves your trust, but standardised analysis of the HD X-ray requires expertise knowledge.

Only competently analysed X-rays are truly of any use. The expert will assess how your dog sits and stands, whether or not his legs are stretched out properly, if he is symmetrical or asymmetrical, and whether the pelvis is even. He will assess the size of the joint space (that is, the gap between the joint ball and socket), and the formation of the joint socket, the femoral head and femoral neck (the part of the thigh just below the joint head), taking into account breed-specific peculiarities of the physique. (For example, Border Collies are more flexible at the hips and ankles than is a bulldog, whose hind legs sit further under the belly.)

He will measure the angle between the centre of the femoral head and the front edge of the acetabulum; the so-called Norberg angle, which is, amongst other indications, one of the most important criteria for the classification of HD. If there are any

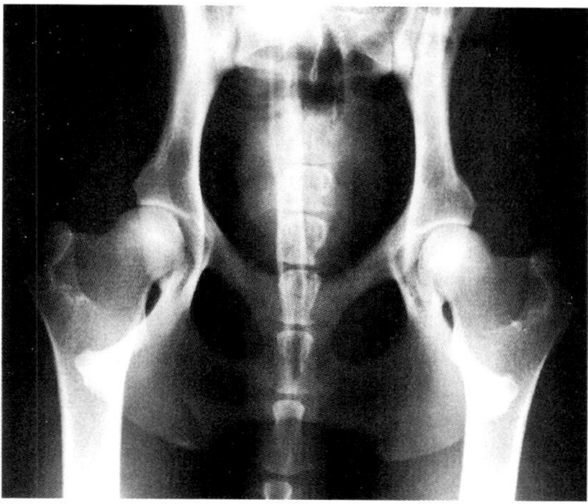

X-ray image of a normal hip joint with no sign of HD. (Courtesy Dr Tellhelm, Giessen)

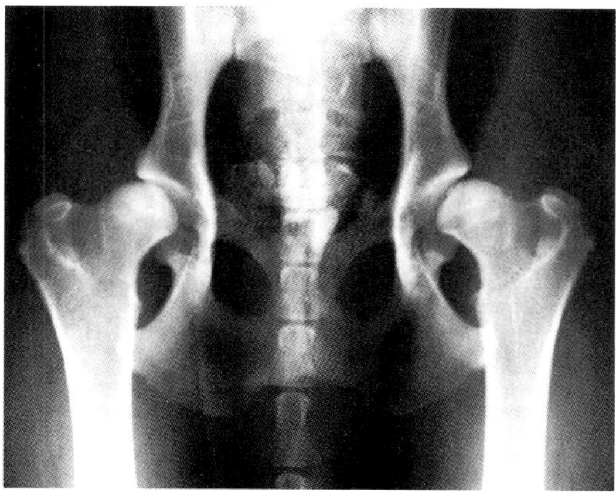

X-ray image of a hip with a diagnosis of 'severe HD.' (Courtesy Dr Tellhelm, Giessen)

changes in the joints (signs of wear and tear, rough patches, and such like), this would also provide an indication of the severity of the HD.

Assessment results range from 'HD-free,' 'suspected HD,' 'mild HD,' 'moderate HD,' or 'severe HD.'

These are not the only definitions; they differ slightly, depending on the breed club. In principle, though, they mean the same thing. For example, joint grading by the OFA is class A (corresponds to HD-free), B (called suspected HD or an intermediate form), C (mild HD), D (moderate), and E (severe). Further subdivisions are also possible, ie A1, A2, B1, B2, etc.

Years ago, a diagnosis of 'severe HD' often meant that a vet would aim to keep the dog as pain-free for as long as possible, and then put him to sleep. Due to a lack of knowledge about the condition, no more could be done. Fortunately, a lot has changed since then, and, while HD is still not curable,some very good treatment options enable an dog with HD to lead a mostly normal life.

Chapter 3

How can I prevent HD in my puppy?

Make sure that any smooth floors in your home, or elsewhere that your puppy will be (parquet, laminate, marble, tile) are non-slip, because slipping and sliding on such surfaces can easily result in over-stretched joints, tendons and ligaments, and therefore injury. This would also cause trauma in the muscles as sprain or muscle strain.

For Kalypso, I covered the relatively smooth brick floor surfaces in the house with carpet. After that, not only was she warmer than on the bare floor, but she could play quite vigorously without slipping.

Of course, a puppy needs to exercise and play. This is important, not only for his mind, but also for his body, as he trains and builds his muscles. Without strong muscles, even the best joints would malfunction eventually.

A puppy can't tolerate long walks. I have seen dog owners who walk for miles along the beach with their puppies. "He's not the slightest bit tired," one owner assured me. This, however, was an illusion. A puppy has no choice but to keep walking with his owner, cost what it may, because he depends on the owner as his guarantee of survival. In a worst case scenario, a puppy would walk until he collapsed from exhaustion.

TIP

Watch for signs of fatigue and take breaks. Six ten-minute walks are better than a sixty-minute walk. Running on soft soil (forest trails, meadows, sand) is better than running on asphalt, stone or concrete. Don't allow your puppy to run after sticks or balls over any great distance.

If you're unsure, ask your vet how much exercise your little puppy actually needs. The general rule for walks is 5 minutes per month in age, so, for example, a six-month-old puppy can be walked for a maximum of 30 minutes.

Sensible nutrition

When Kalypso came to us at eight weeks old, the breeder provided me with a detailed feeding plan, and a list of foods that the puppy had successfully tolerated so far. The list included apple and banana, porridge, meat, chicken, cottage cheese, and yogurt, amongst other foods, and included everything which can today be found in the BARF food plan. (BARF stands for Bones and Raw Food Diet.) Supporters of raw feeding believe that the natural diet of raw meat, bones, and organs is superior nutritionally to highly processed commercial pet food. They replicate a similar diet for their canine companion in the belief that a balanced raw diet will result in a healthier coat, cleaner teeth and fresher breath, reduced stool volume and odour, and better overall health.

As my puppy had a great appetite, and possessed an unshakeable digestive system, it was easy to weigh the ingredients of her meals, mix them together, and simply put the bowl in front of her.

If you would like to feed your puppy this way, make sure you do it safely. Consult your veterinarian about which supplements may be required. He will get to know your dog, his development and his health, and can properly assess your dog's requirements.

Proper management of food intake is a crucial factor when dealing with joint disease.

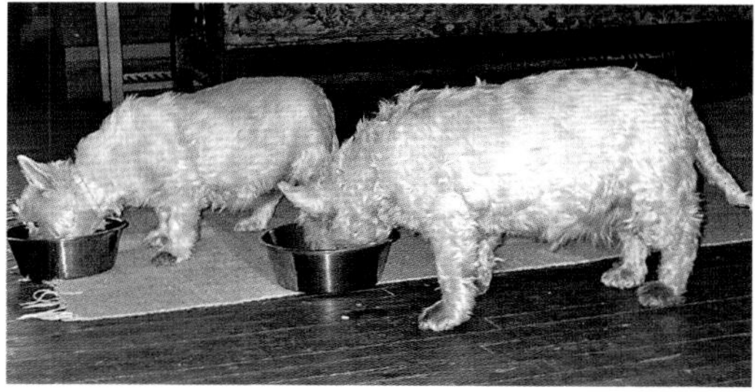

If this special diet plan is not financially viable for you, or if you or the vet have any reservations about it, choose a prepared food. If the breeder has been feeding the puppy with a certain food, then stick to this type. But if you need to change this food, avoid problems by introducing the new food bit by bit, mixing a little of the new food with the old, and gradually increasing the ratio until, after two to three weeks, the changeover is complete.

Consider that there are not only different food manufacturers but also:

- food for different ages
- food for different breeds

A puppy's food and nutritional requirements are different to those of a senior dog, or a pregnant bitch, and a large dog will need a different diet to a little Yorkie.

I fed Kalypso a home-made diet for more than a year, but then, due to time pressures, had to switch her to a prepared food.

Whatever you choose to do, it's important that you manage your dog's weight through strict portion control. Ask your vet how much your dog should weigh, and ensure that you weigh him regularly to keep an eye on his weight.

Whether you call it puppy fat or love handles, every extra gram is more strain on the joints of your dog. The most important rule for the health of your dog is do not

> **TIP**
> When Kalypso was small, I would tuck her under my arm and weigh her with me on the bathroom scales. I then weighed just myself., subtracting my weight from the joint figure to work out how heavy she was. Once she was fully grown, though, we had to use the scale at the vets.

let your dog go too far over his recommended ideal weight (your vet can tell you what this is).

Yes, it's true that most dogs appear always to be hungry, especially if you are in the kitchen. They are hungry when you're eating, or even when you open a tin of cat food. Yes, dogs can beg and make your heart melt. Yes, your dog may look at you in the most heart-breakingly beseeching way but don't be taken in. And don't 'accidentally' drop a morsel on the floor, either ...

A dog can very quickly learn how to prise a snack out of you (by pressing his muzzle against your leg, or forlorny pushing his empty bowl along the floor), and it's tempting to give in, because "he is still hungry," or just "so cute." Your four-legged friend will learn extremely quickly how to train his people to become feeding machines for him. And that's not cute, that's manipulation! Don't give in!

Important!
For the sake of his health, be strict about what you feed your dog.

Keeping trim (or losing weight)

- weigh your dog regularly
- when stroking or brushing your dog, check that you can feel the his ribs and spine, and that they're not concealed under a layer of fat

If the food dummy is not for you, and you prefer to feed your dog once or twice a day from a bowl, no problem. Stick with your usual way of feeding and rewarding, but remember to adjust the amount of food given in the bowl to take into account that given as a reward.

Praise and reward are very important, but, so that his calorie intake doesn't get out of hand, and to ensure the rewards are never boring, I switch between different methods with my dog.

- after saying "good boy!" I immediately produce a small toy from my pocket, to play tug with, or ...
- as if by magic, conjure up a

The food dummy is ideally suited to portion control when rewarding your dog.

TIP

If you have ever partaken in dog training, you know what a great idea it is to reward your dog as often as necessary, although still within his daily food allowance. The food dummy (a bag with food inside) makes very good substitute 'prey' which your dog can search for, fetch, but cannot help himself to. Only you can tear open the Velcro closure, undo the zip underneath, and, if your dog is sitting quietly, give him his reward. The exercise section of this book includes games which involve the food dummy. In addition, there are lots of other games you can play without using this.

In the section *Useful accessories* you can find further information about this. However, please ensure that you supervise him while he has the food dummy as some dogs have been known to swallow them whole!

Rewards do not always have to be in the form of food. Toys are a great calorie-free substitute!

ball and throw it a few feet, so he can fetch it and chew on it with enthusiasm, until he has to give it back, or ...

- I get him to sit and wait and then hide a toy that he can search for when I give him the signal, or ...
- I run a bit with him, and when we stop, I give him a quick cuddle (sometimes he looks at me like a fourteen-year-old boy whose mother has just kissed him in front of all his friends!)

However, Argos doesn't get effusive praise or treats after every good performance. Sometimes, I praise him with a friendly 'well done.' It's only when he learns something new that he gets a proper reward. If he has completed his new task perfectly a few times, then I will begin to reward him every other time, then every third

TIP

Whilst I reward myself for my work at the end of each month, my dog earns his daily ration of food throughout the day. He doesn't get dog treats or chocolate goodies, but, after a good performance, he is given a few scraps of dry food. He finds it very satisfying to hunt for his treats, so I hide them carefully around the room.

or fourth time, and finally only occasionally.

If Argos got a reward at regular intervals, eg, after every third time, he might only do as required every third time because he'd know it was then that he was due something tasty. If, however, he's never sure when – or if – he will get a reward for a good performance, it motivates him to keep working, thinking "Oooh, maybe this time I'll get a treat!"

Sensible training

Sensible training and regular exercise will strengthen the muscles, ligaments and tendons of your dog, and build and maintain endurance and performance, which is extremely beneficial, of course.

Don't allow your dog to race wildly up steps (but see Tip, opposite); neither should he hop or jump up them as this will harm his joints, ligaments, and bones. Instead, controlled slow stair climbing (on a lead) is advised – down as well as up (see photos, right, and also text page 16).

Watch your dog carefully to ensure he is walking and not hopping, or having to make a huge effort to climb each step. His harness will enable you to keep him under good control.

If your house or flat is spread over several levels, allocate a particular floor for your dog, and prevent him from going down or

Opposite: A properly fitting harness is the best and kindest way to walk with and control your dog. There's a great variety to choose from that are both practical and attractive, like the one in the top pictures. The harness below is a canine 'seatbelt' for use when travelling: a special strap attaches to the D-ring on the back of the harness, and then goes around the car seatbelt when it is clipped in place. The chest strap is padded to absorb shock and minimise the risk of chest injury in an accident. Of course, this harness can also be used when walking with your dog.

TIP

Right from the word go, let your healthy dog walk down stairs – this will provide good exercise, and it saves your back if you don't have to carry him. The idea of not allowing your dog to walk up and down steps is now considered an outdated one, and your dog can climb stairs from early in his puppyhood as long as a few rules are observed.

The steps should be the right height so that your dog can go up or come down using one leg at a time without bouncing, or straining himself. Walk your dog by your side on a short lead or harness, and make sure that you both take smooth, deliberate steps. (Of course, when choosing the perfect harness, ensure you take into account your dog's size: a large dog will need a different type of harness to a small puppy.)

up the stairs by blocking them. A child's stair gate is ideal for this purpose (see *Useful accessories*).

If your dog is allowed to climb stairs after surgery, make sure you do this in a completely controlled manner as part of his exercise programme. Incidentally, it wouldn't hurt if you perhaps go out of your way to climb stairs with him – you might not need that gym membership, then!

Incorporate a training plan into your dog's regular walks. This sounds more complicated than it is, as it simply means following these three rules: warm-up – exercise – cool down.

If your dog is raring to go before you've even opened the door of your car, then you will need to make sure he goes carefully during his warm-up. This means spending a few minutes walking more slowly than normal. Once your dog's muscles have warmed up, he can begin doing his training exercises.

Each outing should end with brisk walking on a lead, which will allow the muscles to cool down. You can then give him a massage using gentle pressure, first from neck to tail over the back and sides, with light pressure, then from top to bottom of the legs – he'll love it! (See *Further reading*.)

The methods used for prevention of HD – sensible training and weight control – apply for the period after surgery as well.

My dog is still young, but he's not a puppy any more – what kind of exercise is safe for him?

One hears again and again how climbing stairs is a total taboo for young dogs. This doesn't have to be the case, however, if you follow the basic rules mentioned; you should also make sure that a young dog climbs stairs in a slow, controlled manner – down as well as up. The stairs should be completely slip-proof. If you have a very small dog, such as a Chihuahua or Maltese, chances are the only way he can reach the next step is by hopping. If this is the case, you should either carry him or, even better, teach him to use a ramp when climbing the stairs (a non-slip, secure panel which runs alongside the steps).

Right from the word go, Kalypso adored playing with other dogs. She was particularly fond of an eight-month-old male dog, and it was lovely to watch the two of them together, as young dogs just can't get enough of playing and socialising. However, they are usually not able to find the right balance and don't seem to realise when enough is enough, so that, even though they may be worn out, they will still be keen to run around. As responsible dog owners, it's up to us to keep an eye on a situation such as this.

The bones and joints of a young dog are still growing, and are therefore far more sensitive than the adult bones of a three- or four-year-old dog. Tiny injuries, caused, for example, by a game of rough-and-tumble with a larger, heavier dog, may go unnoticed at first, but they all add up over time, and can lead to more severe problems in the future. To ensure that a game with other dogs doesn't physically overload your puppy, you may need to intervene. Ensure he takes breaks, calm the excitement by distracting him, eg take him for a gentle stroll on a lead for a little while. Breaks like this need not be boring, however, if you give your dog quiet little exercises and tasks to do. This also applies when you take him for a walk: despite the exciting and distracting things going on around him, your dog can learn to focus on you, if he is trained:

- ask your dog to 'sit' and then walk completely around him. Praise him if he remains still
- say 'stay' and stand over your dog. Again, praise him if he remains still
- try a search game. Your dog should remain sitting while you create a scent trail by pulling a morsel of food on a string along the ground, and then hide it in the grass. Now, lead your dog to the beginning of the scent trail and let him search for the treat
- ask him to 'stay' (meaning lie still), even when everyone else is running around. Praise him effusively for this (as a precaution, keep one foot on the lead)

Are dog exercise classes suitable for puppies?

Most exercise clubs for dogs run a 'puppy class' (a kind of puppy school or a playgroup for puppies). Go there with your puppy to check out the place and have a look around. You will probably be able to observe classes, and will see that you and your dog could have a lot of fun in a group like this! In addition, you will make knowledgeable contacts, pick up tips, and have the opportunity to exchange experiences with other owners.

Important!
Your puppy will best learn social skills among his peers. If conflict arises, the group leader will use expert judgement to intervene before a situation escalates. What's more, he or she can ensure that your puppy is not over-worked during the class.

Discover what sports, games or fun groups are offered beyond the puppy age as well. Depending on your tastes and the growing capabilities of your dog, you can choose a class, safe in the knowledge that you are doing something great for your dog.

Which type of activity is suitable?

Choose a basic course for beginners, which will be followed by an obedience exam.

If you have your dog examined for HD, the veterinarian will explain the results of the assessment, and you will know where you stand. If your dog is HD-free, or HD is only suspected at this stage, there are no restrictions on the choice of sports activities. The most important thing is to keep your dog slim, fit and healthy, and watch carefully for any changes or deterioration, in which case, a further check-up will be required.

Chapter 4

The results indicate mild to moderate HD: what now?

Regular visits to the vet will be necessary, as he or she will be your most important point of contact for information and advice on your dog's condition.

If your dog has been diagnosed with moderate HD, it is important that he stays fit, and has strong, stable muscles.

Absolutely off limits are:

- abrupt changes in direction
- sudden stops
- side-stepping/zig-zagging
- jumping too high
- violent, jerky movements

If your dog wants to race around, make sure that he warms up properly beforehand. When muscles, tendons and ligaments are warmed, it helps to prevent injury. Don't hesitate to intervene if a game becomes too boisterous.

Obstacle courses and tight slalom runs can be problematic. Does the exercise club that you take your dog to offer classes where he doesn't have to jump over obstacles, or wind his way around tightly packed slalom bars? Or perhaps the class could be modified to his needs by getting him to go between every other pole on the slalom run, or making the obstacles higher so that he can run underneath them, rather than jumping over them? If the class is not training for a competition, you should be free to decide which exercises your dog can join in, and which ones it's better to give a miss.

Ask if you can observe a group obedience class and watch what happens. For this special type of training, traditional obedience

TIP

Talk to the trainers about your dog's particular handicap. Maybe you could look for a class which focuses on the individual health problems of each dog? This could involve rehabilitation or an activity group for dogs with disabilities. And if no such group exists, why not start one?

techniques are used. Exercises such as searching and retrieving come in many variations, so it never gets boring for the dog. Participants don't work so much on speed, but, instead, the emphasis is on exact execution, so this may be the perfect activity for you and your dog. Activities involving scent-tracking are also ideal.

You could even invite a dog physiotherapist along to the group to explain a few basics, answer questions, and provide information about appropriate training.

Whether or not your pet has HD, swimming is an ideal exercise. The water will support his body weight, allowing him to train his muscles without putting too much stress on the joints. Give him the opportunity

Retrieving and scent-tracking are great ways to train the muscles without putting too much stress on the hip joints.

Swimming is ideal for training the muscles without putting any stress on the joints.

> TIP
> Some cities have swimming pools for dogs. You could also buy your own dog swimming pool, though these are more suitable for smaller dogs. It's a good idea (and much cheaper) to set up the old paddling pool which your grown-up kids no longer use: pull a squeaky toy along on a string in the water, which your dog can only get by swimming after it. Of course, how long he stays in depends on the temperature outside, as well as that of the water.

to swim as often as possible, weather permitting.

Does a dog instinctively know what is good for him?

Some people say, "Leave the dog be – he knows what is good for him. He will follow his instincts."

Troll is a seven-year-old Weimaraner with severe HD, who seems to instinctively know what he

Case history

ANGIE

Angie, an Australian Shepherd bitch, has been diagnosed with moderate HD. She and her owner discovered the perfect solution – not only do they live near a lake, but there is also a local water exercise group. Although this group is primarily for Newfoundlands, Angie is allowed to join in because she works hard, is a quick learner, and has a dedicated owner.

can manage, and what he can't. If he wants to play with other dogs, that's fine.

If there's a tree trunk and he wants to jump over it – sure, why not?

Today he can only run slowly – no problem.

The answer to the question of whether or not a dog instinctively knows what will cause him pain, is not a simple yes or no, as it all depends on the individual. Troll was never particularly daring; even as a young dog, he had a way about him that, in a person, would be described as 'prudent' or 'sensible.' If you are lucky enough to share your life with such a dog, be thankful.

But, just as very few people are lucky enough to win the lottery, not many people live with a dog who is 'prudent.' For example, Carlos, a Labrador, dashes around all over the place, then will suddenly crash into something, emit a cry of pain, and need consoling. The level-headed qualities of the Weimaraner, Troll, are clearly somewhat lacking in Carlos! Impulse control does not really work for him. Deliberation and moderation are the most important methods his owner has to practise, for the sake of his health.

The temperament of your four-legged friend probably lies somewhere between the extremes of Troll and Carlos. If you have observed him long enough in a variety of situations, and know him well, then and only then can you judge when to leave him be to race around in high spirits, or when to whistle him to you, put him back on the lead, and calm him.

Keep a close eye on your dog, and, if in any doubt about what is right for him, consult your vet or an experienced canine physiotherapist for advice.

Why are the muscles so important?

Joints are held in place not only by connective tissue and ligaments, but also by the muscles that surround them.

Imagine for a moment that, from birth, the joint socket is too weak to hold the femoral head in place. Now, if the surrounding muscles are also weak, they can't hold the femoral head in position, either, and allow it to slip out of the socket. This slippage is called a luxation (dislocation). If the femoral head slips only slightly out of the socket, this is called a subluxation.

Strong muscles help prevent the hip joint from wearing prematurely. This wear and tear causes conditions such as arthritis, osteoarthritis, and, of course, pain. (See page 7: *What's wrong exactly?*) Consequently, muscle building and maintaining muscle are important factors in the prevention of HD.

What else can I do?

Ask your vet about dietary supplements. For example, products containing green-lipped mussel extract have been proven to help stabilise tendons, ligaments and joints, and prevent arthritis.

Your vet knows your dog, his disease and his physical condition. He may also know other experts who can help your dog, such as a canine physiotherapist.

Why does my dog need a canine physiotherapist?

Have you ever been treated by a physiotherapist, or received another type of therapy such as manual therapy, active and passive motion therapy, lymph drainage, laser therapy, or electrotherapy? These treatments can be just as effective for us bipeds as for our animals, and it's great that we now have more opportunity than ever to help our dogs.

A canine physiotherapist will not only treat specific diseases, both before and after surgery, but will also advise on different approaches to walking and exercising your dog, and show you all kinds of useful exercises, suitable training methods, and tips for an effective, yet harmless, workout. He or she may even give you 'homework' to do, such as exercises or massage techniques to practice with your dog.

You may be able to do some training with your dog on the underwater treadmill, supervised by the physiotherapist. Many pet physiotherapists offer aqua-jogging, because it's a brilliant way to stimulate the muscles without stressing the joints. (For more on the underwater treadmill, see the section *Aqua-jogging rehabilitation programme* on page 54.)

So, how do you go about finding an experienced pet physiotherapist? You could try asking other dog owners (for example, in a dog class) for a recommendation, or your vet, as he or she is bound to know of a therapist in the area. You can also visit the website for The Institute of Registered Veterinary and Animal Physiotherapists (http://www.irvap.org.uk).

Of course, you can find one via the Yellow Pages or the internet, although it's preferable to contact one that has been personally recommended to you.

How can I tell if my dog has HD, or if his mild HD has become more severe?

So, maybe you decided not to have your dog's hip joints X-rayed, and would like to know if there are any particular symptoms that point to HD? Unfortunately, there are no clear-cut signs, as such, that a dog has HD, but some symptoms can indicate canine HD. If you spot any

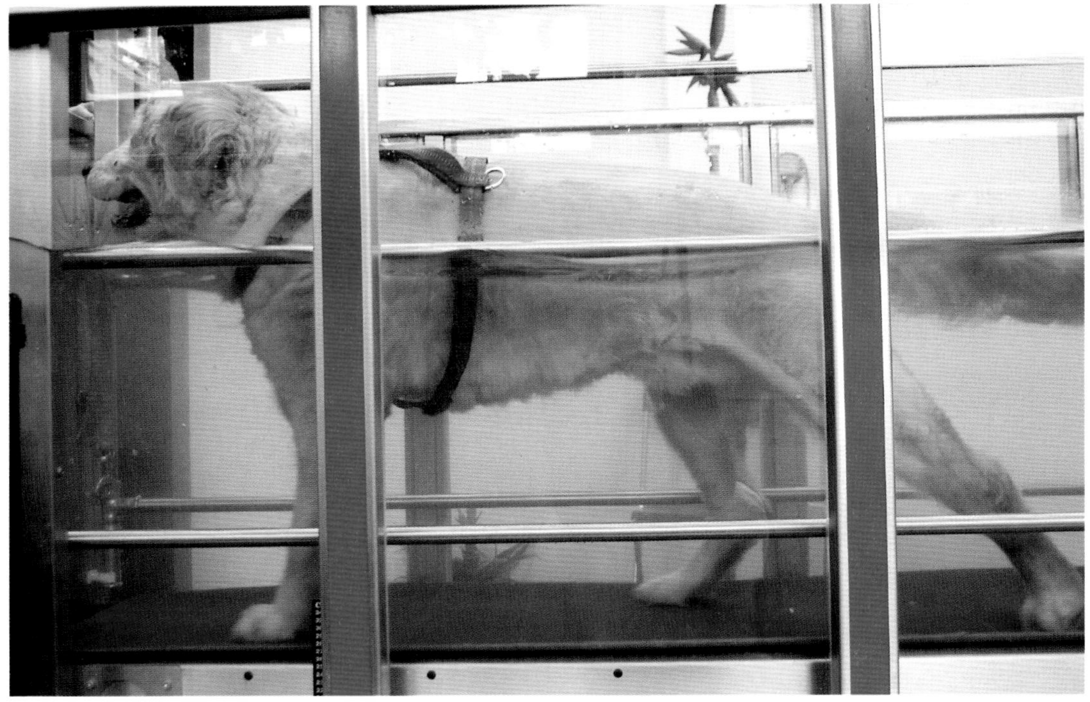

An underwater treadmill is a great way to improve your dog's fitness without putting any stress on his joints.

of these in your dog, please consult your vet:

- if your dog is limping, dragging a leg behind him, and/or maybe it is sensitive to the touch
- if he slips on smooth surfaces or ice
- if your dog takes a long time to bed down for a nap, or stands up extremely slowly and is stiff-legged when walking
- if your dog is limping significantly after playing (possibly only on one side)
- if he is 'flying out of the curve' during a run-around, because his hip has buckled
- if you notice that he runs in a strange fashion
- if his bottom swings from side to side very obviously when he is walking
- if he doesn't want to play when he usually would
- if he goes out of his way to avoid stairs
- if he has trouble jumping into the car, or running up a slope
- if damp weather conditions adversely affect him

The most important thing is this: if you suspect your dog is in pain, take him straight away to the vet to have him checked out.

Remember: persistent pain not only makes a person irritable and short-tempered, it can do the same for a dog. If your dog is in pain, he may respond sullenly, seem irritated, or even growl, which can be an indication of pain on movement, or to the touch.

Pain can also be indicated by changes in the coat, such as tufts of hair sticking up for no apparent reason.

If a dog can no longer lift his hind leg to urinate, this a clear sign that his hindquarters are weak.

Chapter 5
Kira's story

Kira is a seven-year-old Doberman bitch. The Bauers took her on four years ago, after the death of her previous owner, and she proved to be a bright, inquisitive, and enthusiastic pet. The weekly dog class was a real treat for her, and she howled for joy every time she arrived at the car park!

Every now and again, when running on the course, she seemed to be limping a little, but this didn't appear to affect her enjoyment.

"Something must be wrong," thought Mrs Bauer. If Kira seemed a bit lame after the course, they let her rest for a day or two afterwards. They also took her to the vet several times.

'Non-specifically lame,' wrote the vet on the tab. An examination (of her shoulders, elbows, knees, etc) didn't reveal anything serious, and Kira was eager to get going once again.

However, the lameness soon got worse. "No wonder, the way she tears about!" thought the Bauers. They reduced her exercise and tried to get her to slow down.

At some point down the line, Kira began to need painkillers; changes in the weather started to affect her, and she needed some time to 'get going' after a nap.

If she took longer than usual to get into the car, Mrs Bauer was patient with her. She thought, "She can't help it, she just needs longer to get in," but Kira was far too young to be suffering with problems like this.

One day, Kira put her front paws on the edge of the car boot but could go no further.

Mrs Bauer bent down toward Kira's hindquarters to help her into the car. As she began to lift her, Kira suddenly turned and snapped at her. Although uninjured, Mrs Bauer was very shocked.

"The knee-jerk reaction to snap at a slight touch indicates a sudden sharp pain in the area," explained the vet when they visited him soon after the incident. He decided to

X-ray Kira under anaesthetic, and eventually diagnosed inflammation of the hip joint as a result of severe HD.

"She has probably been trying to avoid the pain for quite some time, and this has caused bad posture," said the vet. "People do this when they are in pain as well. Over time, poor posture leads to certain muscle groups becoming stressed and tense, evidenced by solid lumps in the muscle." He showed the Bauers how to feel where Kira's muscles were tight.

"If she hadn't snapped, I wouldn't have noticed anything was wrong, and she would've been in even more pain," said Mrs Bauer. "We didn't know anything about HD."

"There's not just one form of HD with uniform symptoms," explained the vet. "The disease develops differently in each dog, and each dog must be treated according to his or her individual needs."

Chapter 6

Worsening symptoms of HD

It's not unusual for a dog diagnosed with severe HD to live a virtually symptom-free life, whilst another dog with mild HD may be in so much pain that his enjoyment of a simple walk is spoiled.

This is because the classification of HD (mild, moderate, severe) tells us only something about the formation of the hip, and nothing about the damage that may have occurred over the course of time, as a result of the incorrectly aligned joint.

So, for example, in the case of mild HD, the femoral head in the joint may be only slightly out of place, but a small area of cartilage has worn excessively. The cartilage layer has been rubbed off and has lost its cushioning ability, allowing bone to rub against bone, which permanently damages the area. Initially, joint mobility is only slightly affected, but the resultant inflammation and swelling is extremely painful.

So, medical examinations don't tell us the whole story, and the daily observations and experiences of the dog owner can provide essential clues and additional information.

Important!
Dogs are incredibly good at enduring pain, and will not acknowledge when something hurts as quickly as a person would, due to phylogenetics of the wolf. A wolf that can't keep up, due to age or illness, will become separated from the pack, and face the prospect of starvation. To run with the pack is essential to survival; an instinct just as deeply ingrained in today's domestic dog. Therefore, dog owners should observe their dogs very carefully for signs that they are in pan: even then, it will sometimes be a while before they appreciate what the problem is.

The Bauers noticed many signs with Kira, but couldn't pinpoint the cause of them. They registered the evidence of a gradual deterioration in Kira's health, but, ultimately, didn't really recognise why this was. Now they are aware of the problem they are properly informed, and so are far more attentive to Kira's needs.

HD isn't curable, and, unfortunately, won't simply go away overnight. Happily, therapy and other treatments can help your dog lead a pain-free life, with reasonably satisfactory mobility.

When seeking the right therapy, your observations of your dog are essential to the therapist. A dog's owners know his temperament, his favourite activities, the things he loves doing – all of which will help to decide the right therapy to keep your dog occupied (physically and mentally), without going overboard. Too much exercise is just as harmful as too little, so it's essential to determine the correct level of activity for each dog.

Chapter 7
What treatments are available?

There are essentially two options, when it comes to treatment, and the choice of method should be decided with your dog's vet and physiotherapist:

- non-invasive
- surgical

Treatment with medication and/or physiotherapy is called non-invasive treatment, and the chapter entitled *What does a canine physiotherapist do?* explains the range of options. In the exercise section, you will find appropriate exercises for your dog and some helpful suggestions. Controlling body weight, or following a strict weight loss regime, is an essential part of any treatment programme.

Apart from active therapy, the physiotherapist may recommend additional measures such as cold/hot packs for pain relief (see *Useful accessories*), and he or she will offer massages for tense muscles, perhaps demonstrating specific massage techniques or showing you how to use a simple massage comb. You could also consider investing in a good book about canine massage, which you can use even when your dog has recovered. (See *Further reading.*)

Medication

The vet may have prescribed painkillers, with advice on how to give them to your dog in order to keep him pain-free, so his HD doesn't result in bad posture. The problem with this is that it will initially mean increased pain for him, because he will put more strain on the body than he would normally bear. This could also cause further damage. Ask your veterinarian about homeopathic remedies for your dog. These are available as:

- drops
- tablets
- globules (which are like beads), or
- small globules (very small beads which have less space between them, make more mass, and soak up more liquid)

Caution!
The active ingredients of homeopathic remedies enter the blood via the oral mucosa (the mucous membrane of the mouth, including the gums). If they are mixed with food, they will not remain long enough in the mouth to be absorbed, and so will not be effective.

Homeopathic tablets and pessaries have a coating made from milk sugar (lactose), which contains the active ingredients.

Caution!
Some dogs are lactose intolerant, and even very small amounts can cause diarrhoea. If you're unsure about how your dog may react, initially try a very small dose to determine whether he can tolerate the tablets or globules. If he gets indigestion, talk to your vet.

Help! How do I give my dog medication?

Administering homeopathic medicine shouldn't be too much of a problem, simply because it doesn't smell or taste unpleasant.

You can crush tablets and pessaries between two teaspoons and, using moistened fingers, apply this to the oral mucosa (inside of the lips, under the tongue, along the gum). If your dog finds this approach a bit strange, you could practice a few times with a tiny dab of liver paste, for example, and a few little treats ("yum, this is nice!") until he gets the idea that your finger in his mouth equates to a nice, tasty treat.

Another option is to smooth some yoghurt over the surface of a bowl, sprinkle the crushed tablets on top, and then allow him to lick the bowl. In this way, the mucous membranes can absorb the active ingredients before they make their way down the oesophagus.

You don't need to crush the globules because they're small enough, and can be administered in the same way as the crushed tablets.

Drops can be given either neat or diluted with a little water using a disposable syringe (without needle) directly into the mouth. If you are unsure about this, practice it a couple of times with a small amount of soup or similar. If the sight of the syringe causes your dog to wag his tail in anticipation, you know you've won!

As for conventional painkillers in tablet form, depending on your dog, these are often not as easy to administer.

Aisha will eat anything, including pieces of bread spread thinly with butter which have a tablet hidden within. Basco will gulp down pills if they are wrapped in a slice of sausage. Argos is so keen on cat food that he doesn't even notice there's a tablet in it! Donna, on the other hand, is not so easily outwitted, and has formulated a clever technique. She will move her mouthful of food around on her tongue until she has isolated the foreign object, and then spit it out.

Sometimes it helps to give your dog four or five identical small pieces of food. Conceal the tablet in the third piece of food. Your dog will eat the first two pieces, and, reassurred that there was nothing untoward hiding in them, will take the third offering with little suspicion, rushing to eat it because you have a delicious fourth snack ready, held high above his head so he has to stretch up to reach it and gobble it down ... easy!

Any tricks are allowed – as long as you keep it friendly!

If nothing seems to work, you may feel frustrated – but talk to your suspicious or hesitant dog in a friendly tone. Reassure him that he is the greatest dog in the world, your absolute favourite, a really lovely, wonderful dog! Here's what to do next.

Have your dog sit next to you, preferably where there's little chance of escape, such as in the kitchen next to the table, on which the tablet is hidden in a small piece of sausage, wrapped in a large portion of cat food, or clamped in a tiny piece of cheese.

Talking reassuringly to your dog the whole time, hold the top of his muzzle and gently lift his upper lips until you can see the space between the upper and lower teeth (A).

Extend your fingers into this gap and gently open his mouth just enough so that you can push the disguised tablet as far back in his throat as possible (B & C).

Hold his head pointing upward (but not too far back as this will scare him), and stroke him gently from the jaw down to the throat to promote swallowing (D).

Praise your dog when he swallows – tell him what a good

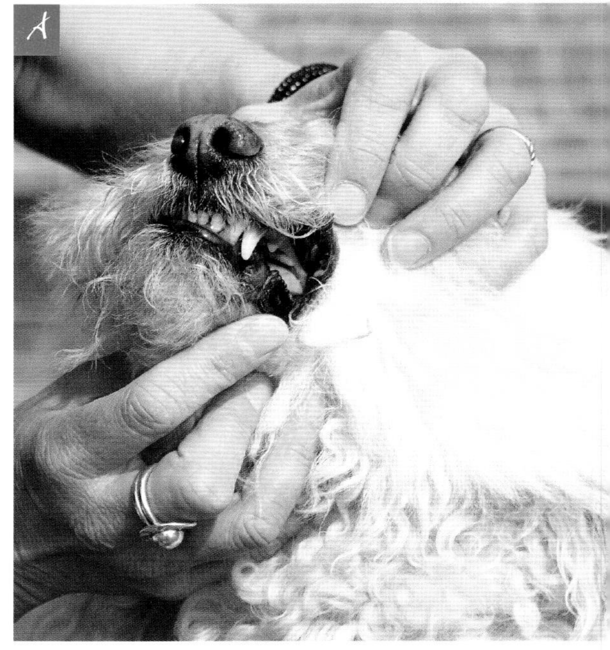

A

B

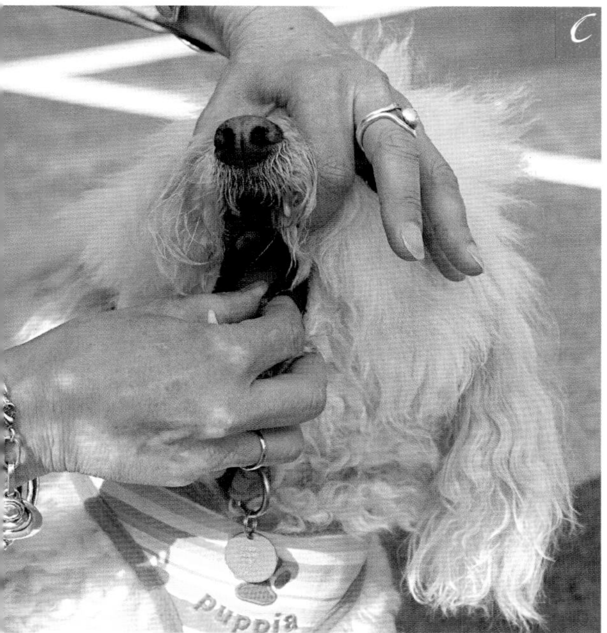

dog he is, and give him an extra treat as a reward.

What operations are available for HD?

There are several different surgical procedures; these are the most common ones:

Triple pelvic osteotomy (TPO)

Triple pelvic osteotomy is a procedure that preserves the natural hip joint, eliminates subluxation (laxity), and prevents the progression of arthritis.

This procedure involves cutting the pelvis in three places and rotating the socket to allow better flexibility of the femoral head (ball portion of the hip joint). The joint will then be more stable and, therefore, pain-free. This is an effective method, so long as the pelvis does not incur any damage during the operation.

Femoral head lengthening (FHL)

This technique is used for dogs whose femoral neck is too short, which means the hip muscles are not able to hold it in place.

As the name of the procedure suggests, the surgeon extends the femoral neck bone so that the femoral head will fit into the hip socket.

All major hip muscles are attached to the so-called greater trochanter of the femur, located in front of the femoral neck. Extension of the femoral neck improves the leverage effect, because the femoral head is pushed into the socket with more force and held with better stability.

Total hip replacement (THR)

This is replacement of the entire hip joint. The surgeon removes the femoral head, neck and acetabular cup, and replaces them with a replica made of surgical steel, titanium, or a specific type of polyethylene.

In the case of a younger dog, the surgeon will only suggest THP when the growth plates have closed (ie when he is fully grown), because otherwise serious problems would arise if the bones have not fully developed.

Gold bead implants

Gold bead implants are a permanent form of acupuncture, intended to alleviate the pain associated with HD, and not an actual treatment for the condition. The gold beads – about the size of a pinhead or tip of a fine ball point pen – are implanted in points on the dog's back and head, and provide long-term stimulation of the points. Using a needle, three gold beads are implanted in each location (which is very precise). If the beads are off even one sixteenth of an inch (slightly less than 1.6 mm), they will not be effective.

Gold is used because it is non-reactive with the body. It is not known exactly how the gold bead implants work. As with all forms of treatment, this method works for some dogs and not others.

Femoral head ostectomy (FHO)

This procedure exposes the head section of the femur bone (the ball of the ball-and-socket joint), which is then removed using a small saw or a bone hammer and chisel. It is rare that both hips are done in one operation – usually, one side is done and allowed to heal, and the other is done at a later date. Unlike most other hip operations, the head of the femur is not replaced, but is allowed to heal and develop its own fibrous scar tissue, so that the joint is no longer bone-on-bone – this is called a pseudoarthrosis (also known as a 'false joint'). The neck of the femur is usually removed at the same time as the head to prevent the post-operative complication of bone rubbing on bone, and continued pain. Dogs who have had FHO surgery are required to maintain a lower body weight throughout their lives to compensate for the loss of skeletal strength, and generally have less mobility than normal.

This operation is very complex and is only carried out as a last resort.

Chapter 8
When the vet advises surgery

If the training, physiotherapy and painkillers aren't sufficient to deal with your dog's HD, your vet may recommend surgery.

He or she will take into consideration not only the degree of impairment and pain, but also your dog's age. For example, it would not be advisable for a 14-year-old dog to undergo a serious surgical procedure, with all the associated risks and possible complications.

Important!
Clarify any outstanding issues. Don't be afraid to ask the vet, surgeon or physiotherapist plenty of questions. Discuss the cost with your family, and only opt for surgery if you are sure that you are able to shoulder the financial burden and time commitment.

What if an operation is not possible?

Paul is a six-year-old German Shepherd cross. He is very friendly, but is an anxious and insecure dog, and no one knows anything about his history. When his owner got him from the shelter two years ago, he was in a pitiful condition. His HD has now caused osteoarthritis. Most likely because of the pain, Paul was not used to moving around very much, and his muscles had atrophied. He was a sad sight to see. With endless amounts of patience, his new owners succeeded in building his confidence, and Paul began to feel relatively safe with them. Through careful training, he was able to build a small amount of muscle mass. He was given painkillers, but couldn't stand very well. His new family wanted him to have an operation, but after long deliberation, decided that Paul would be too psychologically traumatised by major surgery.

As an alternative, they decided to try gold bead implants (see Chapter 7). Although slightly sceptical of this, Paul's owners wanted to leave no stone unturned, so researched the internet, spoke to veterinarians and dog owners with personal experience

Case history

KIRA

Kira is a quiet but active seven-year-old Doberman with HD, whose owners – Mr and Mrs Bauer – have decided that surgery is the best way forward for her.

"I have no experience in this field," their vet told them, "so I'll give you the contact details of a specialist." Accordingly, the couple made an appointment with the orthopaedic surgeon.

The surgeon read the notes, looked at the X-rays, examined Kira, and finally advised a total hip replacement (THR). He justified his reasons for choosing this method, and explained the operation details.

Finally, the three discussed the anticipated financial expenses. As well as operating costs, medication and physiotherapy following the surgery will incur additional expense.

Through a series of recommendations, the Bauers went to see a canine physiotherapist to discuss treatment and the cost of it. They wanted to do everything they could for Kira, but had to be sure they were able to afford the treatment.

We recommend you use the time before the operation to make contact with a canine physiotherapist. She or he can give you helpful tips in advance, and your dog will have the opportunity to become familiar with the new environment.

of the method, and finally found a therapist who was familiar with the process.

In fact, since having this treatment, Paul needs almost no pain medication. For the next stage of his treatment, his owners want to take him to hydrotherapy classes, introducing each new idea slowly, so as not to overwhelm Paul with too many new things at once.

Tomorrow is the day of the operation

The vet has advised that your dog should fast before you take him to the clinic. As a precaution, check when his last meal should be and when he should stop drinking water, prior to the operation. Be sure to follow your vet's instructions to the letter!

But why must your poor dog starve? Surely he has suffered enough already?

Of course, he is not really suffering, only temporarily going without food. The fact that most dogs will do anything to get food is due to their basic survival instincts (eat now, while there's something to eat as who knows when the next meal will be?). If you follow your vet's instructions, nothing terrible will happen – on the contrary, this will keep him from harm.

Why is this strict fasting necessary?

Your dog will be given a general anaesthetic, which may cause him to feel, or actually be, sick. If he has food in his stomach whilst unconscious, he may suddenly vomit. He won't be able to get up, like he can when he's sick on the living room carpet, and adapt his breathing. Therefore, there's a very real risk that he may choke on his own vomit. Should this happen, the surgeon might be able to abort the operation in time to avoid the worst – but maybe not. In any case, such a scenario puts a considerable strain on the dog. And, of course, the practicalities are that the surgeon will have to cancel the operation, book another appointment, administer another anaesthetic, etc, etc … and your vet probably won't be very happy, either …

So, fasting really does mean fasting! You will feel terrible as your dog stares sadly into his empty bowl, but stay strong, and make sure that the rest of your family supports you with this. For your dog's sake, please don't be tempted to give him 'just one treat'; it could well be his last if you do.

After the operation

So, the operation has gone well, and now you can collect your dog. If you've not already done so, you will need to sort out how you will transport him home. Ask the surgery if he is still very drowsy, and what sort of behaviour you should expect (extreme fatigue, apathy, loss of appetite, etc), and over what period of time. Clarify how often the dressing should be changed, and make an appointment to do this.

All dogs are different, of course, and may react in various ways. For example, Aisha had no appetite and wanted to be left alone. All she could manage was a few steps to the nearest patch of grass to do her business.

Argos was quite different. He wanted to be near me, languishing in self-pity, and looking as if he was half-starved and generally neglected. He kept leaning against my leg, his posture emanating very deep sorrow.

Getting back to normal

You may find that small family members, in the mistaken belief that it will help, will lie down next to your dog, stroking and touching him, feeling sorry for the poor, dear creature, and giving him tidbits.

Pampering like this is counter-productive, however. You may even find that your dog has previously hidden thespian talents, and really gets into the role of tragic hero, bribing you to feed him lots of treats, which will eventually ruin his health.

Of course, your dog has been through the ordeal of an operation – but he doesn't need pity, only for his family to treat him as they usually do, with lots of love, care and respect. You don't need to compensate for his (temporary) lack of joie de vivre. Similarly, you don't have to reward him with extra treats because he has had an operation.

The less fuss you make, the more likely it is that your dog will feel that things are normal. Simply do whatever is necessary to help him heal: make sure he's not in pain, is not hungry or thirsty, or suffering from boredom.

More medication

"Does Aisha really have to take painkillers? She's bound to get used to them after a while and then they will have no effect."

"What if he ends up addicted to the painkillers?"

"I am apprehensive about the many side effects of the tablets, all of which are listed on the packet! How can I do this to my little dog?"

"Pain is a necessary part of life, isn't it?"

The ability to feel pain is essential for survival. Picture the following situation: a bubbling saucepan full of chicken soup, giving off tempting smells which your dog just can't resist. He starts drooling with anticipation, gets his front paws up on the stove, and begins lapping up the soup, which he gulps down. The resultant burns and internal injuries would be pretty horrific.

Pain can prevent these and other injuries from occurring: pain protects him because it warns him in advance that something is wrong. In the case of the soup on the stove, the warning is: "ouch – hot – stay away!"

However, long-term pain can cause a huge amount of stress, over and above the everyday, the-children-are-driving-me-mad and I-never-have-time-to-do-anything kind of stress. Persistent pain causes a kind of stress that negatively affects the entire body and, for example, upsets and disrupts metabolism. It can suppress the immune system, reduce respiratory function, and interfere with wound healing – to name just a few side effects.

Aisha, Argos, Basco, and Chico should experience as little pain as possible, not only because pain is unpleasant, and because no one

You are allowed to feel sorry for your dog after his operation, but don't overwhelm him with treats and attention.

wants their beloved pet to suffer needlessly, but also because chronic pain in animals has hugely negative biological consequences.

Another important factor: if Kira's leg is causing her pain, she won't want to move about. Without painkillers, she would only get up for the most essential things, and then retreat quickly back onto her blanket. Argos would do the same because he doesn't want to suffer any unnecessary pain. When dogs are injured, they are usually very quiet, unassuming patients, and easy to care for, though unwilling to exercise if in pain – not for all the love in the world! But it's exercise which will help them heal over the coming weeks.

Muscles can be built – or rebuilt – only by repeated resistance training; that means regular training of the muscles or muscle groups, using guided, purposeful movement.

If you find a movement or action very painful, you probably won't want to do it – so why should your dog? However, you are responsible for helping your dog do the exercises that the physiotherapist and the vet will recommend to you, as well as ensuring that he is not in pain. Give him the painkillers prescribed by the vet – they are essential to the success of your efforts and rehabilitation measures. And as he gradually recovers, progressively discontinue his painkillers.

Your vet will give you instructions for administering painkillers, and will advise how long the effects of the drugs given during and after the procedure will last, when you should start giving your dog painkillers, how many, and at what time intervals. It is important to follow his instructions to the letter, to ensure that your dog is as pain-free as possible.

On the lead

Your vet will have advised that you keep your dog on a lead whilst out (and just a one metre lead at that!), and walk only short distances, such as to and from the local shops. Stay away from other dogs to avoid joyful reunions. Let doggie friends know about your dog's impending operation so that they understand why you can only greet them from a distance.

It is very important to prevent your dog from jumping into the car. Jumping out of the car or from somewhere high (chair, low walls, table, etc) is also off limits, as it will place stress on the front legs, shoulder, and all other joints. And remember: because your dog will favour his hind legs, the front legs will have to do more than normal anyway.

Now may be a good time to get a car ramp (see *Useful accessories*), as this will not only be a big help with getting your dog into and out of the car, it also means that grooming can be done on a table instead of on the floor. At the same time, with the non-slip board, you've also got a training aid for uphill running.

Maybe your dog is a small Yorkie whose favourite spot is on the sofa ... from now on, jumping from places such as the sofa, bed, or chair is prohibited. Lift your little

TIP

Give your dog his morning dose of painkiller well before the first walk, so that it has plenty of time to take effect before you go out. The vet can tell you how long this is likely to be, and for how long each dose will be effective, which will allow you to determine the best time to take your dog for a gentle walk.

dog up or down, get him used to lying on a cosy dog mattress on the floor, or provide him with a small ramp (see *Useful accessories*).

Finding a canine physiotherapist

Seek out a canine physiotherapist in your area and have a chat with him or her. Generally speaking, you will receive a recommendation for physiotherapy treatment from your vet or the surgeon after your pet has been discharged.

So, now you're bound to be wondering, why is physiotherapy so important? Any interference with a joint puts stress on all involved tissue structures. During the operation, the surgeon will have moved or stretched muscles, tendons and ligaments (and also removed the remains of the damaged cruciate ligament); the joint capsule will have been opened, and so on. Following surgery, structures and tissue in the area will be traumatised: a violation such as this sets off a chain reaction in the body, which needs to be treated and then gently worked to restore performance. This speeds up the healing process and minimises any damage.

Introduce your dog to the physiotherapist slowly, without causing him any stress or anxiety about the new environment. He should get to know the therapist ("nice lady") and become familiar with the practice ("smells like dog-interesting stuff"). When, later, he has his operation, after all the strange new things that have happened, he will have something familiar that will help to rebuild his trust in the world again.

During the familiarisation process the therapist may lead him to the trampoline or the fabric tunnel, for example, give him a chance to sniff everything, and maybe have a go on one or two things. He might enjoy it so much that, after his operation and after the stitches have been removed, he looks forward to going back to this fun, (dog-)friendly place.

It is also reassuring for you to know that your dog will be in good hands.

The physiotherapist will tell you what to expect in terms of therapy costs. If you budget your time and money, you'll be able to plan your next steps for the weeks after the operation.

Since you must now limit the length of the walks you take, it's important that your dog is exercised passively. Passive motion stimulates the metabolism in all tissues involved in movement, and promotes blood circulation. Improved blood circulation supplies the cells with more nutrients, which, in turn, helps prevent stiffening of the joint capsule. Again, a good book such as *The Complete Dog Massage Manual*, published by Hubble and Hattie, has all the relevant information about this technique.

To be on the safe side, ask the physiotherapist to show you how to support your dog without causing any harm during passive movement massage.

Nutrition

Due to the necessary exercise restrictions, your dog's calorie requirements will decrease, and he'll need less food. Your vet can advise on the best way to reduce food intake, without causing any nutrient deficiency in your dog.

Remember to ask for products containing green-lipped mussel

Cracky has a new hip joint.

Case history

CRACKY

Cracky is a three-year-old Labrador, who has been X-rayed because of a gastrointestinal illness. The pictures are clear, the abdomen is easy to see, but there is an irregularity in the hip. The vet suggests, for safety's sake, a thorough examination of the hips.

The X-rays of the hips show Grade C HD on the right, and Grade D HD on the left. Naturally, Cracky's owners are very shocked. Alarmed by this surprising finding, they watch him very carefully when he playing and exercising, yet can't see anything remarkable. In the autumn, however, when the weather turns cold, Cracky is clearly limping, and, in the morning and after long naps, has a lot of difficulty getting up.

Owner and vet weigh up the different options. Cracky is given light muscle training and NSAIDs (non steroidal anti-inflammatory drugs – these are painkillers without cortisone, which are used in the treatment of rheumatism). Eventually, Cracky gets a new hip joint. Following the operation, his recovery is overseen by a canine physiotherapist.

> TIP
> Can you replace part of his food allowance with apple slices, pear or carrots? Perhaps you can make extra-thick, extra-hard baked wholemeal biscuits, using copious amounts of apple or carrot in the mixture?

extract – this helps to slow the onset or worsening of osteoarthritis, and is beneficial for tendons, ligaments and joints.

Fill a large Kong® toy with food (for more on this, see *Useful accessories*). Your dog will have to use his brain to figure out how to get the food, and this will occupy him for some time. Again, he is having to work for his reward. Use cottage cheese with apple, pear or grated carrots instead of calorie-laden foods such as peanut butter.

Aisha's owner has a food processor in which, every morning, she processes apples, pears, cabbage, and/or carrots. The mixture is kept in a jar in the fridge, so she always has a low-calorie treat available. Sometimes she fills the Kong® with apple and carrot gratings and a spoonful of low fat cottage cheese, so that she doesn't feel as if she is depriving her dog!

Kong®: mentally and physically stimulating for your dog.

Chapter 9

What is the role of a canine physiotherapist?

Each therapist has different treatment methods, but usually, the first visit will go something like this.

He or she will give your dog a chance get to know him or her (to sniff), if they have not yet been introduced, go through your dog's history, and ask some questions –

- what is the history of the HD?
- what procedure was used in the operation and when?
- who did the operation?
- who is your dog's vet and what are the contact details in case of any medical issues?
- does your dog have any other health problems, such as allergies, intolerances, etc?

The physiotherapist will analyse

Case history

KIRA

Practically every day Mrs Bauer recorded on the computer which exercises worked well for Kira (very good, average, poor, a lot of effort required, or easy, etc), what Kira had improved on, and what she still couldn't manage. For example, for the first time after the surgery, Kira tried to balance or walk on a tree trunk, which she always used to be able to manage very well, but could now manage only a few wobbly steps. Over the next few days, Kira's owners had her walk along benches instead of tree trunks. After some practice, Kira finally managed to move two, then three metres along a tree trunk.

n Kira's diary Mrs Bauer kept a record of which exercises Kira was very reluctant to do, or couldn't do; there had to be a reason for this, and her notes and observations gave important clues as to how the therapy should progress.

your dog's gait, which means studying how he runs, if he runs without difficulty, or whether he has a limp. He or she may then –

- weigh the dog
- measure his leg circumference in order to assess the existing muscle, so that progress or setbacks can be evaluated
- test muscle response and assesses balance
- consult with you about treatment and a training plan
- show you how to keep a training diary

A training diary doesn't require much effort, but does allow comparison of progress made week to week. It also makes it easy to see where any problems may lie, and what you need to practice more with your dog.

Chapter 10
Care and activity during the rest period

Your dog probably won't enjoy being inactive. If Basco has nothing to keep him amused in his waking hours, he soon becomes bored. A dog who doesn't have enough to keep him busy may feel unhappy, depressed, irritated, grumpy, or rebellious. Or he may try to amuse himself – which is rarely to the liking of his humans!

Goldie, a five-year-old Labrador bitch, turned her attention to the legs of some antique furniture to relieve her boredom. Gecko, a six-year-old sheep dog cross, ripped off part of the wallpaper and carefully removed the carpet strips on the living room floor.

Dogs need something to keep them occupied and, immediately after the operation, a variety of exercises and mental challenges. It is important that you give your dog something to do. Aisha, for example, finds foraging for food highly satisfactory.

Here are some game ideas:

- let your dog search for toys which have been hidden in the house, put food scraps in a sealed toilet roll, or hide them behind half-open doors
- hide a treat under a saucepan lid and see if he can lift the lid to get it
- put some scraps of food in an old sock, close it with a rubber band and hide it – your dog must find the sock and bring it you before he (every second or third time) gets a treat out of it. Have him sit before sending him to search for it, then sit again when he gives you the sock – the action of sitting/standing, standing/sitting will strengthen his muscles

Could your dog learn something new? Perhaps a trick, which you can perfect indoors? You could rehearse for a show at the next children's party, or Grandma's 80th birthday; for example:

- teach your dog to pull off your socks, gloves, or cardigan (use old items to practice with)
- if he can bark on command,

Many household items are ideal to use in 'find' games.

During his recovery time you could teach your dog all sorts of useful tricks, such as how to put his toys away, as well as get them out!

practice the trick 'my dog can count'

- teach him which container is the bone, ball, or treat hidden in?
- sit on the floor and let your dog search for a toy concealed in your sleeves, trouser leg, pocket, etc
- teach him the 'touch' trick, where he has to touch different objects with his nose: your hand, the ball, the door ... you could even get him to operate a light switch
- he could learn to pick up and carry things in a basket, such as the newspaper or letters from the doormat
- he could put socks and other small items of clothing in the washing machine
- how about if every toy has a name so you can ask him to bring Kong®, bring Teddy, bring the ball, the duck, the frisbee, etc

Rico was trained by his mistress to bring 77 different objects. After he had a shoulder operation at the age of nine months, he needed to rest. In order to challenge him mentally, his owner began to teach him various words. Within nine years, he could recognise about two hundred words.

Of course, not every dog will be able to do this, but Rico's example shows you how you can put your dog's mental capacity to good use and keep him occupied at the same time. Dogs need stimulation so that they don't become depressed or bored.

You can also buy or make intelligence games for dogs; see *Useful accessories*, where you will find information for some game ideas.

You could also fill the Kong® with tasty, low-calorie treats, which he will spend some time getting out.

Get your dog moving – this is

This 'treat ball' is just the thing to provide mental and a little controlled physical stimulation for your dog. He'll love pushing it around with his nose, trying to get the treats to drop out!

Before taking your dog outside for a walk, hide some tasty treats along the route, and let him sniff them out! Very rewarding for him – and a great way to engage him, mentally and physically.

important for his heart, circulation, muscles – and his soul. The vet will have prescribed strict rules regarding on-lead exercise only, so your dog is still not allowed to run or jump, or play with his canine friends for the time being.

Just how much your dog can do depends on the surgical procedure undertaken and the healing process. Talk to your vet and/or physiotherapist about this, ensuring that you follow their instructions.

Chapter 11
What can the physiotherapist do to help?

The physiotherapist offers a range of techniques to treat your dog according to his needs, to promote healing, build muscle, strengthen ligaments, and relieve tension. He or she will also explain and demonstrate which of these techniques you can use at home, and how to do them safely. And you may even be able to borrow some equipment to do the exercises at home.

The most commonly used techniques used are:

Massage
Massage is very relaxing, relieves tension, and thereby eliminates muscle pain. Toning techniques encourage blood circulation and increase oxygen supply to the muscles. One massage technique, effleurage, is particularly good at helping to re-establish mobility.

Heat therapy
Heat improves circulation, increases metabolism, and relaxes the

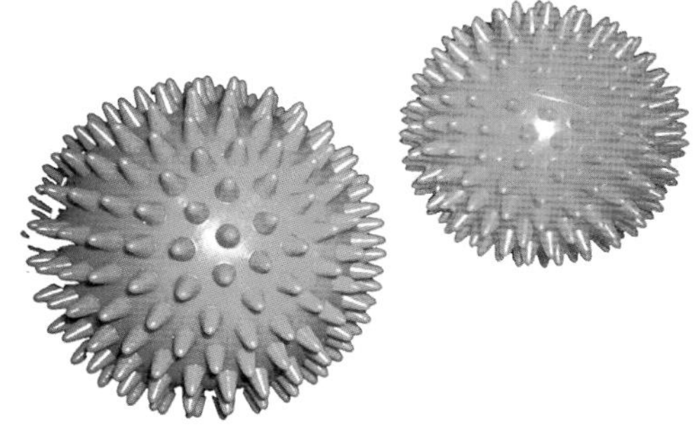

A hedgehog ball is a good massage tool.

muscles. It will also make the connective tissue (eg joint capsules) more flexible, which increases mobility. The physiotherapist uses infrared lamps or hot packs (see *Useful accessories*) before exercise therapy.

Cold therapy
Reduces swelling and inflammation (for cold packs, see *Useful accessories*).

Ultrasound therapy
While hot packs and infrared

Your hands should form a soft and uniform shape during effleurage.

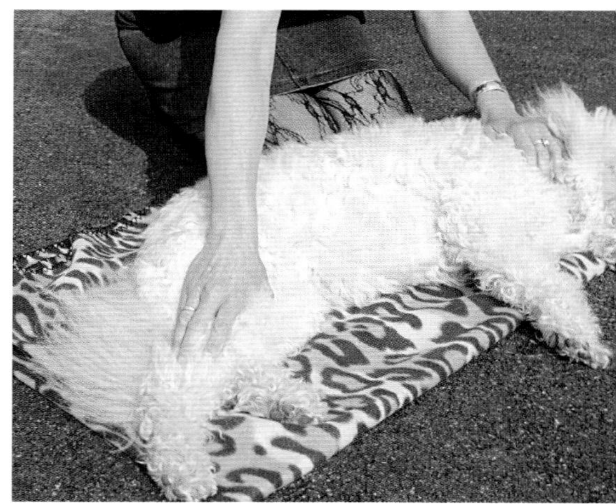

The positive influence that massage has on the circulatory system can help promote healing.

radiation heat the outer layer of the body, ultrasound reaches the deeper layers. The heat generated there reduces muscle tension and pain, and improves circulation, which in turn speeds up the healing process. This therapy improves joint function, and some of the existing stiffness will ease. Depending on the sound intensity used, penetration depth is 1-5cm, which will have a beneficial effect on the joint capsule.

Electro-therapy (TENS)

TENS (Transcutaneous Electrical Nerve Stimulation) stimulates the skin using mild electrical impulses on the nerves, and blocks pain signals before they can be received by the brain. You may have seen this device already in your physiotherapist's practice, as it is also used on humans. During a treatment, you will see that the muscle in your dog's leg gently twitches, possibly relieving tension and easing pain, allowing him to relax enough to doze for a while. These minimal movements help build

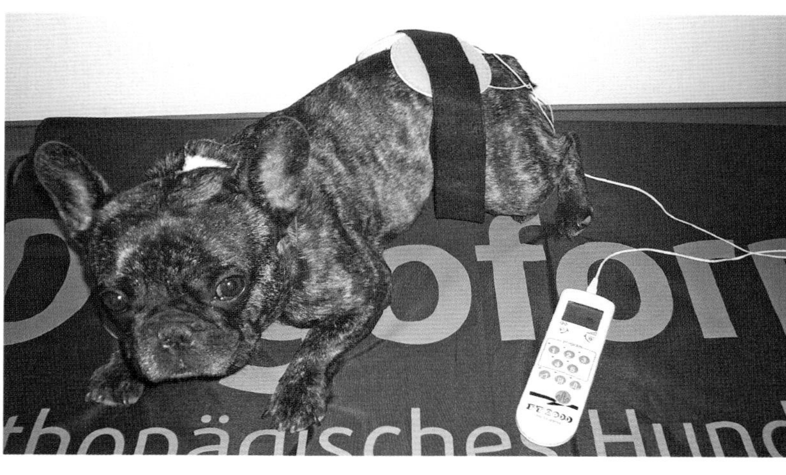

TENS therapy stimulates the nerves using mild electrical impulses.

new muscle tissue, and thus prevent muscular atrophy (muscle wasting). At the same time, the process will regenerate nerve tissue and bone.

Due to a small change in posture and unnatural weight-bearing, Aisha has tension in her back. You probably know how this feels if you have ever suffered from backache: it hurts.

Dogs howl if they feel a sudden pain. With longer-lasting pain, however, they suffer in silence, and, unlike us, can't say where it hurts. If the physiotherapist can reduce or completely eliminate muscle tightness by applying brief electrical stimulation, this is such a relief for Aisha.

It's possible you may be able to borrow this piece of equipment to treat your dog at home.

Additional applications for this type of stimulation range from muscle strengthening to therapy for paralysis. These treatments should, however, only be carried out by a trained physiotherapist.

Low-level laser therapy – intensive light therapy

The high energy laser light used in this treatment penetrates the subcutaneous layers of skin, and works deep down in the muscles, which provides pain relief and improves circulation. It also stimulates the metabolism, which means that by-products of inflammation, such as toxins, are removed from the cells more efficiently.

If your dog has an oedema (an accumulation of fluid in the tissue), laser therapy reduces swelling,

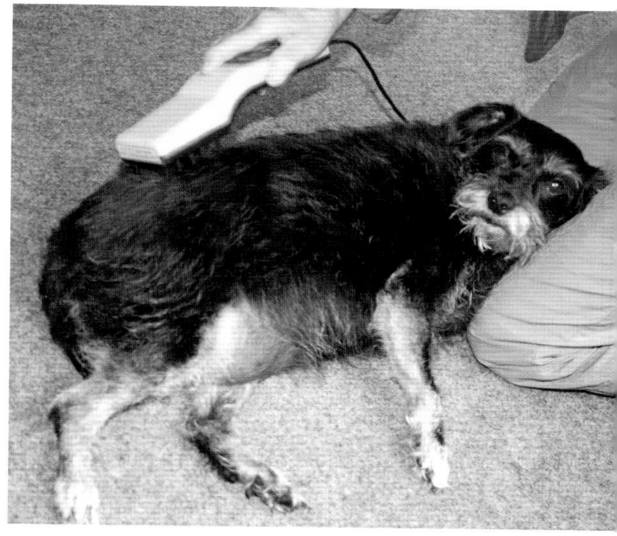

Laser therapy is relaxing, reduces pain, and improves circulation.

because it aids lymphatic circulation and lymphatic drainage. In addition, the laser light is directed at certain acupuncture points, which aids the healing process. Laser therapy is also used to heal scar tissue.

Exercise therapy (active and passive)

For active exercise therapy, the therapist designs exercises for the dog which require movement of specific, individual muscles and muscle groups. In passive motion therapy, the dog does not move of his own volition; the therapist moves parts of his body – such as paws or legs – for him.

The ultimate aim of exercise therapy is pain-free mobility of the dog, or, at the very least, to maintain and build muscle, give him the desire to move (again), and create and improve physical fitness and endurance.

Exercising on an underwater treadmill strengthens your dog's joints and muscles and improves his posture and gait.

Aquatherapy

If you've ever done water aerobics you'll know why it's so good for you – the buoyancy of the water means your joints are protected, and you almost feel weightless. A dog experiences the same thing during aquatherapy.

The pressure of the water also acts as gentle lymphatic drainage, and therefore reduces swelling. Water resistance promotes muscle growth, and if the physiotherapist turns on the jet stream for a few minutes, your dog will love it!

Water pressure provides resistance, improves circulation, and boosts the metabolism, which will all help your dog to heal quicker.

Scar treatment is a major concern for the physiotherapist. Why? Well, to a dog, scars are probably of no great importance, but scar tissue is less elastic than normal skin, and it may be lumpy and hard. This can cause problems such as:

- itching and inflammation

If a scar itches, your dog may try to gnaw on it, and it may become infected as a result. Your dog may need to wear an 'Elizabethan collar' after his operation

- pain

Scar tissue is less flexible than the underlying layers of skin. With movement, the flexibility of the different layers vary – normal skin is elastic, while scar tissue is more rigid, which can cause your dog a lot of pain

- licking

When dogs lick their skin, they can cause eczema. Many people believe that dog saliva is healthy, when, in fact, it's quite the opposite! And because the skin stays damp from licking, it's an ideal breeding ground for all sorts of pathogens

- raised scars

The thicker the scars, the more of a problem they become, because of their inflexibility and low elasticity, and the increased risk of pain, leakage, etc

- allergic reaction to suture materials

Just like people, dogs can be allergic to a substance – even to the stitches which hold the wound together. This will obviously hinder the natural healing process. The physiotherapist will help to identify such an allergic reaction early on, so you can be advised about what to do next

- encapsulation of residual suture material

If the 'seam' of the wound is not fully knitted together, the body's immune system will try to encapsulate the stitches in order to break them down. Ultrasound therapy and/or an intense scar massage will help the body reabsorb the suture faster

The physiotherapist will massage the scar with the aim of achieving optimal flexibility in the skin tissue, and giving pain relief. She will show you how to do this so you can help the wound heal successfully

Chapter 12

After the stitches have been removed

Does my dog still need his medication?

Yes, definitely. Building muscle and exercise training are only possible if your dog is mostly pain-free. Discuss this with your vet, and also ask about possible alternatives, such as homeopathic remedies.

As previously mentioned, food supplements containing green-lipped mussel extract help to prevent the development of osteoarthritis. Make sure that your dog's food contains enough high quality protein, which builds muscles. Each dog needs a different amount, depending on his age and general health, so ask your vet for his or her recommendations.

Caution!

Dogs cannot digest raw egg whites – you're better off using these to bake coconut macaroons, but only for your human family members!

Off the lead – what now?

At last, the vet has decided that the wound has healed. But that doesn't mean your dog can race out of the house, jumping for joy! All of the new-old movements must be tackled in a calm and measured manner:

- ask your vet how long you can walk with your dog, at what point you may extend this time, and by how many minutes
- watch your dog as he walks or trots beside you, and keep an eye on whether he limps to protect one leg (which one is this?)

Gradually, you'll be able to walk for longer, and eventually you can go jogging with your dog. You might even be able to cycle slowly on your bike, while your dog accompanies you alongside. However, he shouldn't be allowed to gallop.

It's tempting to involve him in a game of frisbee at your local park, and let him enthusiastically greet all his old doggie mates, but please supervise him closely at all times, to make sure he doesn't get hurt.

With your dog on an extending lead, walk 20-30 paces away, and stop. Without looking at your dog, simply wait ...

... until she comes to you, sits, and makes eye contact with you.

Obedience problems after a long time on a short lead

Sometimes the period of rest can seem too long for a dog, especially if he has always had a strong urge to be active, and a rich and eventful social life. You may be amazed to find that bad manners have suddenly appeared from nowhere: for example, Goldie pretends not to hear the usual whistle, and has developed a sudden penchant for hunting.

The following is an example of an exercise you can use from time to time if your dog is in very high spirits.

Put your dog on a 5-metre long lead. Not looking at him take 20-30 steps in one direction, stand still, and still do not look at him (which would otherwise be an invitation to play, and he must earn this first). Wait until your dog comes to you, sits down and makes eye contact – and at that exact moment say "good" and maybe play tug of war with a toy, or toss him a little treat.

Once he has finished the treat, take (again without eye contact) 20 to 30 steps in a different direction, stand still, wait until he sits and watches, then praise him, and play a quick game or give him a little treat – and so on, again and again.

If you're standing still and your dog won't come to you, wait 30 seconds and walk 20-30 steps again. Sooner or later, he will come over to investigate! Pretty soon, he will realise that if he doesn't sit still and look at you, then nothing nice will happen!

If your dog barks, it may be he is trying to persuade you to play, or give him something to do, or whatever. In this case, stay silent and just ignore him, look in another direction or, even better, turn your back on him and move on until he is quiet. If he is quiet and sits and looks at you, then play a quick game or give him a treat.

After a while, your dog should begin to understand the ritual, and so you can play for a little longer; maybe let him play with a ball (but no further than the length of the lead), or run for a little distance with him. A word of praise will increase his motivation and willingness to focus on you ("When will she finally give in?"). He doesn't want to miss a play session or a morsel of food, but he never knows when or if it will happen.

As soon as he shows signs of wanting to be off the lead, immediately put him back on a short lead and walk briskly with him, with sudden turns, and tight corners, asking him to 'heel' and 'sit' along the way.

Once he has calmed down, put him back on the long lead.

Granted, you may sometimes feel like a Sergeant Major, but the only way to ensure that your dog re-learns his obedience training is by being consistent and persistent (you are allowed to sigh here!).

Above all, ensure you keep your dog busy with a variety of exercises such as dog-dancing, search games and scent-tracking games (see *Useful accessories*) – activities that demand his full attention. This should demonstrate to your dog that it is much more fun spending time with you than trying to run off.

Get your dog's attention – and calm her at the same time – by walking briskly on a short lead, making sudden turns, and asking her to 'sit' and 'heel.'

He will get plenty of exercise and his mind will be kept active.

Of course, it may be difficult to retrain a dog that has just been 'released,' and you may feel sorry for him, thinking: "He just wants to have his freedom ... enjoy life ... run around properly like he used to." But if you let these bad manners become a part of everyday life, it will be very difficult afterwards to regain your authority and convert the bad habits, however understandable they may be, to acceptable behaviour.

Quite apart from that, chasing buses is a very dangerous activity ...

and humid smells tempting. But what a large tank full of water, technical stuff everywhere, and strange noises! Aisha is extremely curious!

Dr Häusler advises at her practice:

"For the first treatment, it is important to reassure the animal and owner alike, because they are both bound to feel anxious and unsure about the new situation. For the first visit, I recommend taking something along for the four-legged patient – this could be a treat or a dearly-loved toy. You could bring a few different things and conjure them out of the bag, so that

Case history

KIRA

Kira loves egg yolk more than anything else, and has one three or four times a week – but she has to work for it! Before her operation, she could sit with her front paws raised to get her treat. After surgery, she learnt to do it again, but with difficulty. Gradually, Kira has managed to build up her strength and can now hold her balance in this position for up to ten seconds.

Aqua-jogging rehabilitation programme

At last, the wounds have healed, the stitches have been removed, and the vet has no objection to a spot of aquatherapy. Perhaps you have heard of the underwater treadmill but aren't quite sure what it is?

After a detailed conversation with the therapist, and possibly an opportunity to explore the actual treadmill, you'll see that it really is quite an impressive device.

Kira loves anything that has to do with water, and finds the warm

your dog considers this occasion exciting and not frightening. The first treatment will vary from dog to dog. Duffy has no reluctance about getting on the treadmill. Dart is completely different – he needs time and lots of encouragement. Dart's mistress finds it frustrating that her dog refuses to climb the steps to the treadmill. 'He's not usually like this,' she complains impatiently.

Rule number one: Keep calm! "It doesn't matter," explains Dr Häusler to her, "Dart is a careful dog, which is a really positive thing. An

Underwater exercises offer many advantages, including greaty improved mobility.

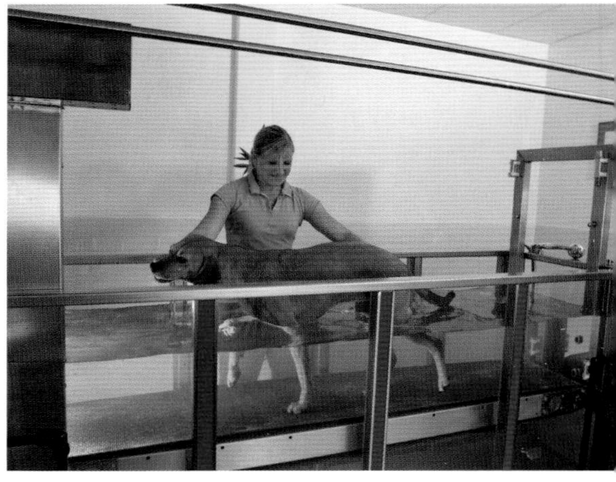

impulsive dog could be in danger of injuring himself. Over time, and with encouragement, his anxiety will lessen; if he comes in stressed and tense then this is counterproductive. A tense body cannot train properly, and could even suffer injury. He would also return home with the impression that this is a nasty place, where he experienced bad things. And next time, he would be in a state of anxiety before he had even got in the door.

"At last, we manage to get Dart on the treadmill. I let it go up first and then move it sideways across the pool. Finally, I let it down very slowly, until Dart has his feet in the water. Friendly persuasion and lots of praise reassure him that everything is okay. Toys and treats are an excellent distraction. Next, I sink the treadmill bit by bit into the water. It is fairly warm, so Dart isn't cold – yet it takes him a while to realise that all these strange things aren't a threat to him.

"The deeper the dog is lowered into the water, the greater the support for his joints. This is all new for him, and he can't control the motion of the treadmill. Gradually, however, he will begin to feel relief from pain. When the treadmill begins to move, he is puzzled at first, and then very soon realises that he can actually run on the strange surface – and is praised effusively for it.

"This first session with the underwater treadmill is not so much about training, but merely to reassure the dog that he will come to no harm. These early experiences are crucial for further therapy sessions. If he decides at the end of the session that it wasn't too terrible, but actually quite fun, next time, he will be happy to participate in the treatment. Even the owners, who had previously believed that their dog was either afraid of water, or was very stubborn, are fully convinced about the benefits of the training after the third or fourth time. Dogs usually notice very quickly what does them good, or can quickly become convinced."

It is fascinating to watch a dog on the underwater treadmill, which allows them to work on many things at once. Their gait is often exaggerated, new muscle groups are engaged, extra balance is required on the treadmill, they are better able to bear weight on their limbs, and the treadmill aids both neuromuscular re-education and agility. The viscosity of the water creates resistance for the muscles, resulting in a great strength and endurance workout.

Summary

So now, you and your dog have a therapist, a treatment programme, and a few weeks of rehab ahead of you. The therapist will go through all the exercises and give you 'homework' to do with your dog. In addition to this, the next part of the book shows you a great collection of do-it-yourself toning exercises that I used for Argos' rehab. These exercises are not intended as a replacement for the highly effective aqua-jogging, but they will show you practical ways you can play with your dog and train him appropriately without wearing him out.

Depending on where you walk (forest or park?), you can choose which exercises you want to do and give them a go. Some exercises are suitable for inside, or for the garden; experiment and see which ones your dog likes best. And remember: your dog doesn't mind whether you call it training, physiotherapy, rehabilitation or physio-homework. He's happy whenever you do something together that's varied and enjoyable.

Chapter 13

Exercise to rebuild muscle

The following exercises are used to build muscle. Your dog should start these before his operation, then his stronger muscles will better support and protect his hips. Start slowly and increase the duration and frequency of the exercise.

Back to basics

After the operation, clarify with the vet when you can begin various exercises with your dog. Although we have included some instructions on how often you should do these exercises, this is intended as a guide only. Every operation is different, and the healing process varies from dog to dog, so it's essential you get advice from your vet.

Of course, your dog will not appreciate that these exercises are for his benefit, so you will have to make them attractive to him.

Encourage him with catchphrases such as "activity time!" which tell him that you will be playing new and exciting games! For most dogs, there can never be enough variety; all new opportunities are welcome and, fortunately, old games, after a few days' break, will seem new again.

Your dog will almost always work for the prospect of a reward, be this praise, attention, or food.

For Basco, who loves games, that can mean fetching a ball or playing a game with a Kong®. Aisha is primarily motivated by treats, so search games involving small treats are ideal for her. She enthusiastically searches for the food dummy and is ecstatic when she is given her treat from it. Vary the accessories and games that you use to keep your dog's interest; two or three are all you need if you swap and change them each time. If the squeaky duck disappears for a few days, and then reappears, it is much more interesting than having it to play with for five consecutive days, morning, noon, and night.

Next, you will need some little food treats, but instead of chew sticks and dog chocolate, use some of your dog's daily food allocation. Aisha and Basco are quite happy to receive dry food as treats from their daily food ration, and this will prevent weight gain.

The food dummy can be used with and without food. It is a durable, sealable bag – you could even make one yourself! (See *Useful accessories.*)

Fill the food dummy with part of the daily food ration – which will vary according to the number of walks/workouts your dog does. If you are taking three walks, each time you go, fill the dummy with a little less than a third of the daily ration; for four walks, a little less than a quarter. Whatever is left over from this portion can be kept in reserve for special treats, until after the last walk in the evening, or when doing additional exercises at home.

It may seem pedantic to divide up the food in this way, but it will help to ensure that you don't overfeed your dog. Aisha has a huge appetite, Basco drools and stares at the food dummy – nearly all dogs are very greedy, and you always have reason to reward your much-loved pet, but your dog shouldn't become overweight as a result.

Every gram of excess food puts unnecessary strain on the body, joints and ligaments. They become overburdened, as does the circulation, thereby reducing your dog's desire to do something new with you and train his muscles.

Being slightly underweight is healthier than being even slightly overweight. Take advantage of every vet visit to get your dog weighed, and ask the vet whether he thinks your dog's weight is okay. If necessary, he will be able to advise you how best to help your dog lose weight.

Ask your vet how long after the operation you can begin with simple exercises, how long your walks should ideally be, and how to extend the time gradually.

The best way to control your dog's movements is to use a chest harness (see *Useful accessories*) to which you can attach a short lead. At the start of the walk, in the warm-up phase, allow him to determine his walking speed – but watch for signs of pain or discomfort. When venturing out for the first time, walking on his 'new' leg will feel really odd to your dog. He will probably be unsure or unsteady at first, so be kind and patient with him. Gently encourage and reassure him by talking to him whilst you are walking.

Hindquarter weight-bearing

Lead your dog to a bench (or a low wall), and place a morsel of food or the food dummy on the edge, so that he can place his front paws on the bench and reach up to the item.

With a small dog use (according to his size) a tree stump, a tree trunk, or possibly a large rock.

If you know that your dog likes to jump up, then hold his harness, and say "stay" while you hold the food just above his nose on the bench, so that his front paws remain on the edge. Now, raise the

TIP

Always have the food dummy to hand whenever you are on the move. Allow your dog to carry it – perhaps to the nearest bank or the next woodpile, or wherever you want to do an exercise during the walk. Have a toy (for example, the Kong®) in your pocket, or put a small toy in the food dummy, which your dog can search for, fetch, and finally play with the contents.

There should always be a reward immediately after a new exercise is performed. Then, to keep it unpredictable, reward him after two or three repetitions, and later, after four, two, five, one, three repetitions. Always give a kind word of praise when he has done something correctly.

If he has done something wrong, ignore his mistake; a cry of "No!" is too negative, and your dog will feel disappointed or discouraged. Simply start again.

Immie has two types of harness. She wears this one when out walking …

… and this one is her safety harness when travelling in a car. A special strap fits around the seatbelt and then attaches to the D-ring (which means, of course, that the harness can also be used when walking).

treat higher so that your dog has to stretch – and possibly even lean backward slightly – to reach his treat.

As your dog stretches for his treat, look at the toes of his hind legs, which should be spread a little as he weight-bears on them. If the toes of only one foot are spread, or neither are, it could be that something hurts, or maybe he's afraid that it might hurt to do this.

TIP

Ask your dog to carry the dummy (with a treat inside) the last 5 or 10 metres towards a bench (or low wall), and drop it on the bench. Have him stand with his front paws on the bench, and hold the dummy above his head, and he should bend quite far forward and then backward (which helps with co-ordination). Open the dummy and hold the treat above his head, so that he leans forward and back again. Finally, give him the treat.

Fetching, dropping, bending forward and back, eating, is an entire exercise sequence that you can vary so that it never becomes boring.

Observe his toes on a regular basis when he does this exercise – you should find after some time that the toes are spread, which is a sign that your dog's legs are getting stronger. You *both* deserve a treat for this!

Argos loves this exercise so much that he will carry the food dummy to every bench he sees, even in the dark, drop the dummy, put his front paws on the bench, and wait for his treat, as if to say "again, please!"

In the forest where we walk, there are tree trunks next to the path. Aisha is encouraged to stand on the tree trunks: front paws on the trunk, back legs on the ground, stretched out as far as she can.

You may sometimes find stacks of logs by the side of the path. Basco walks along one of the lower logs and likes to stretch up to investigate the next log. Encourage your dog to stretch a little higher and for a little longer by offering a treat. Don't actually allow him to climb the log pile, of course, he

A low tree stump is suitable for helping to improve weight-bearing on the hindquarters. Try this exercise for a few seconds at a time initially, and gradually increase the duration.

How high can your dog reach up the tree when he stands on his hind legs? This game is ideal for strengthening his hindquarters.

On a woodpile, different stresses are applied to each leg, which will help him to relearn proprioperception.

should simply stretch up. Encourage him to do this by holding treats just within his reach.

If the benches start to become boring, find a tree with very rough bark, such as a pine tree. Estimate how far your dog can reach up the tree when standing on his hind legs, and lodge a treat in the bark at this level. He then has to search for his treat. If he has to scratch or gnaw on the bark to get the treat between his teeth, that's great, as he will give his legs a good workout – and you should both find this exercise quite enjoyable. Getting him to stand up on his hind legs may not be easy, but it's worth it, for the sake of his muscles.

If he gets the idea that some trees have treats in the bark, when you lead him towards the next tree, he will investigate by standing upright against the tree and leaning to the right and left, because something smells tasty – which is the perfect way to strengthen his legs. Put a morsel of food on a branch, wedge the dummy in the bark, or hide a few crumbs in a hole in the tree. You can increase the length of time he stands upright by putting something on the bark which he can lick off – perhaps a piece of banana or a dollop of wet food.

If your dog loves scentwork, use a piece of kibble (dry meat or fish) in the tree, and drag the food dummy along a track while your dog is otherwise occupied. Lead your dog to the start of the track, say "find" and let him follow the track and reach up the tree as high as he can until he finds what he's looking for.

There are other ways that trees can be used as exercise aids. Try this one – for which you will need a toy with a rope attached to it – two or three months after surgery. Hang the rope on a branch, and allow the ball to dangle temptingly from the tree. Check the height – if your dog can reach up to the ball while standing with his hind legs slightly bent, it is in the right place. Ask him to get the ball; make it seem very exciting. If he retrieves the ball, give him lots of praise, but if he's been trying for a while without success, ask him to sit and then praise him for being so good! I can always tell if Argos has had enough because he sits down and looks at me, as if to say, "Well, I can't get it – you try!" So end the game before your dog becomes frustrated or bored. If he has happy memories, he will be pleased to play the game again.

Caution!

I had the bright idea of extending the rope using the lead, leaving the ball dangling over a ladder rung, while I held the lead from behind the ladder. So far, so good – my dog pulled at the ball, I pulled at the lead, and he pulled and growled and fought. Great. Until he suddenly let go of the ball and I fell on the ground with a thud! If you play tug

Training on the physio-ball.

Playing tug of war with front legs off the ground.

of war with your dog in this way, please be aware of what might happen!

Hindquarter flexibility

With your dog standing face-to-face in front of you, attract and hold his attention with a toy held above his nose. Move it gradually forward over his head toward his hindquarters, and he should bend his hindlegs, as if to sit down – this is precisely the moment where you praise him.

This half-squat position is hard to teach and hard to learn, because dogs prefer to sit, which they are more accustomed to. If it doesn't work, then it doesn't matter; there are plenty of other exercises you can do instead. But if it works, get your dog to hold this position for 2 or 3 seconds – great!

Have your dog stand facing a bench, and throw some treats underneath it. To look under the bench to locate the treats your dog will have to bend down on his front legs, and then bend his hind legs, too, to get to the treats. So that he doesn't just lie down, get down with him and hold his stomach off the floor with your hands underneath him. After a few repetitions, he will understand what's required.

Using a treat, encourage your dog to creep halfway under the bench, then tempt him with a toy, which he should try to grab and pull out from under the bench. Once he has the toy in his mouth, gradually loosen your grip on it. Just before he's about to give up. let him have the 'prize' and praise him.

In this exercise, Argos tries to

The half-sitting position – virtually a squat – is a great workout for the hindquarters, but initially difficult for the dog to learn.

Crawling under a bench requires good co-ordination and is suitable only for experienced patients. If your dog is reluctant to do this, please do not try and force him.

TIP
If you have already used a clicker, you will know that you can 'tell' your dog exactly what you want him to do with it. If not, see *Useful accessories* for more information.

fool me by lying down on the ground and then sliding under the bench. I don't give him his treat – instead, I push my toes under his tummy so that he can't get comfortable and has to hold himself up with his leg muscles.

When running through the tunnel, your dog will have to bend his hindquarters, which will strengthen his muscles.

Through the tunnel
Tunnels (fabric tubes) are ideal for your dog to run through. It's better if he can't run with his head held up, but has to crawl instead, which is a great exercise for his leg muscles.

If you don't have a tunnel, ask your dog to crawl under a bench or under the sofa, chair or, better still, several chairs in a row. Or you could form a tunnel with your legs and get him to go through it (sit on the floor and put your legs or feet up on the sofa, or sit on the edge of a chair with your knees bent to make a tunnel).

If you have children, have them stand one behind the other and create a tunnel with their legs. Your dog can run through the tunnel and your children can gradually make that tunnel smaller and smaller so he has to crouch to get through.

Balance exercises
After surgery, your dog needs to strengthen his muscles and train his reflexes. Balance exercises will improve his proprioperception (the sense of spatial awareness and limb positioning).

With regard to your own body, you will automatically know, for example, whether your leg is straight or bent; you're not even aware of thinking about this as it is done subconsciously. Without proprioperception, body control and co-ordination would not be possible: not for gymnasts, ordinary people, or other animals.

After the operation, your dog's proprioperception will be a little confused. With Kira, this was very noticeable: after the operation, she couldn't balance on a log like she could before, and her owner had to slowly help her learn proprioperception all over again. At first, Mrs Bauer got her to walk on thick branches with very rough bark (so that she wouldn't slip), while she stayed close by, ready to catch her if he fell.

Practising balance on a log.

Log piles are ideal for training canine muscles and re-learning proprioperception.

Caution!

Safety first, as always! Ensure your dog doesn't slip and become frightened, anxious, insecure or injured.

Your dog will understand best what you want from him if you teach him using treats and lots of patience. For example, going back to the log piles, if they aren't too high, just let your dog investigate them. Hide a little treat in-between the logs so that your dog has to balance on his hind legs to sniff it out. Walking back and forth along the logs and sniffing for his treat will improve his strength and balance. Stay close to him in case he panics or slips, though.

Is your dog small to medium in size? If you have a mini trampoline, see if he will jump on it. Let him climb carefully onto the trampoline (for a very small dog, use a board as a ramp). It may take him a while to adjust to the different surface, which will seem very strange at first. Give him time. He will eventually get used to it and maybe begin to enjoy this unusual exercise!

Can you encourage him to stay on the trampoline for a little while? Fantastic. Make sure you give your four-legged friend lots of praise!

Can you get him to walk a few steps on the trampoline? With food in your hand to tempt him, and with patience and plenty of praise, see if he will walk round and round the trampoline, clockwise and vice versa – great! Really praise him if he is willing to do this.

After Kira had become familiar with standing on the trampoline, Mrs Bauer carefully climbed on, too, and bounced a little. Kira had to balance to stay upright. The following isometric exercises can be done either on or off the trampoline.

Isometric exercise

Isometric exercise, or isometrics, are a type of strength training in which the joint angle and muscle length do not change during contraction (compared to concentric or eccentric contractions, called dynamic/isotonic movements). Isometrics are done in static positions, rather than being dynamic through a range of motion. The joint and muscle are either worked against an immovable force (overcoming isometric), or are held in a static position while opposed by resistance (yielding isometric).

Do you maybe have a mini trampoline your dog can use?

Examples of this are pushing or pulling an immovable object like a wall, or a bar anchored to the floor. Although research shows that isometric exercise increases muscle strength significantly, it doesn't change the length of the muscles. Today, it is primarily used for rehabilitation purposes. The exercises strengthen the muscles and train the reflexes: you can use these on a healthy dog to help prevent hip dysplasia, for example, and also with a dog who has had surgery, to strengthen his muscles after treatment.

Here's an example of such an exercise:

With your dog standing in front of you, place one hand flat

TIP

This simple exercise will help your dog feel at home again in his own body.

Ask your dog to sit and ask for first one paw, then the other. Keep alternating the paws and this will help him regain his balance and build his confidence.

on his right thigh, and the other on his right shoulder. Now, with both hands press gently against his body. You only need enough force so that your dog resists the pressure to prevent himself from falling over. Your dog stays on the same spot, using his muscles to resist the pressure of your hands. Holding this position, slowly count to five, gradually let the pressure subside and praise your dog. Carry out this exercise three times in a row, several times a day, swap hand positions; that's it! This is a good exercise to add to your rehab programme: doing this on the trampoline makes it slightly more challenging as your dog has to retain his balance as well as resist the pressure.

Standing on three legs

Make sure your dog is standing on firm ground, then lift one leg at a time and hold for a few seconds (ask your vet or physiotherapist to show you how to do this safely). You can do the same on the trampoline, but please ensure that your dog isn't anxious and is able to keep his balance.

Slow steps

Walk your dog at a very slow pace, which will ensure that he uses all of his legs and can't leave out his weakest leg. The best time to do this is after he has done a few other exercises or been for a walk. Put your dog on a short lead and walk slowly enough that he can't break into a trot.

The smaller the dog, the more difficult this will be as he will be more likely to break into a trot.

Walking uphill

At first, only practice walking uphill sparingly, and don't increase this until you have achieved some progress with your dog's training. As a precaution, ask your physiotherapist or consult with your veterinarian for advice on this.

Good places to practice uphill walking are small – or even large – banks, for example. Keep your dog on a short lead, in case he tries to charge up the hill. Also, walking up a ramp but be sure to stay right beside him in case he should seem unsteady.

Walking uphill requires more muscle power, so you may prefer to use a faster gait. You'll see that your dog walks uphill with a high, curved back – this powerful force exerted by his muscles is a great workout for him. Vary the exercise by going straight up a few times, then diagonally or zigzag. This not only strengthens the muscles of your dog, it will 'feed'

TIP

Allow your dog to run on soft surfaces as often as possible: in meadows and in the forest, on soil, sand, and through snow. If you are near the sea or have a stream nearby, this is also good, but only if the surgical wound has completely healed.

If you have access to a schooling ring (inside or outside), take him there as the floor is usually the ideal surface (wood shavings, sand, or a sand and fabric blend, wood chips, etc) on which to walk your dog.

his nerves with information about proprioperception.

Also vary the pace – and the place you do this – but always ensure that your dog remains in step with you.

Inclined plane

An inclined plane (a dog ramp, for example) can be used in many ways, and is an excellent way to help your dog into the car or onto the sofa, plus it will train his hindquarters. As you can see from the photo below, the dog has to take long strides with his hindlegs to cover the length of the board. The change in gradient means that the weight bears on his hindquarters, so ensure that you are close by to help should he slip, which could well result in injury.

Slow, tight turns are good for weight-bearing on the injured limb, and also improve coordination.

A car access ramp can be used as an inclined plane for training the hindquarters. Ensure that it is wide enough, and safely secured so that it does not slip.

Tight turns

These can be part of the warm-up routine. They help to ease tension in the back, and necessitate your dog using the muscles in his hindlegs. Tight turns also indicate hindleg condition: if the dog sets his weight squarely on all four paws, he's fine, or at least improving: if his weight is not evenly distributed, this could indicate bad posture or that he is in pain.

Exercises on the trot

Begin at a walking pace until your dog falls into step with you.

- walk in a straight line with him

- walk him through a widely spaced slalom (maybe around trees or molehills ...)
- walk a couple of figure of eights around the molehills!

Walking backwards

If your dog is unfamiliar with this (as I expect most dogs will be), begin by walking alongside a fence. After a few metres, stop walking and hold a morsel of food above his nose and slightly over his back. His first reaction may be to sit down, so prevent him from doing this by holding his harness up a little. He should then take a backward step in order to reach his treat. Give him his treat straightaway and lots of praise. Repeat this again, until he takes a few steps backward. It doesn't matter what word you use for this; you can simply say 'back' or 'backward,' for example.

Dancing bear

Here's how to do this –

- have your dog sit facing you
- kneel in front of him and gently lift both front feet off the ground and then replace
- do this a couple of times until he is quite used to it
- lift the paws a little higher so that your dog is almost upright
- if he's happy with this, take a step or two backward, and then forward, with your dog following you each time
- give him plenty of praise!

Climbing steps

This is a good exercise to strengthen the hindquarters. Begin slowly with low steps and, as your dog's strength increases, progress to steeper steps. Put him on a short lead and harness so you can ensure that he uses controlled movements only.

Caution!

Check that your dog lifts each of his paws properly, step by step, and doesn't leave out a particular leg, or jump or hop.

Sit-and-stand exercises

Whilst on a walk, ask your dog to sit and then get up again quickly, which will exercise and train the hip and knee extensor muscles. While he is sitting, check whether both hindlegs are in the same position, or if he is extending one leg to the side. If he extends his left leg to the side, walk him with the left side of his body close to a wall, then have him sit close to the wall so that he can't stretch out the left leg. Praise him when he's sitting correctly, even if he does so only because the wall prevents him from extending the leg.

Tell your physiotherapist if he extends a particular leg to the side, because she will know what to do in order to avoid or lessen any permanent deformity.

Lifting the paws

When your dog walks, he should lift his feet properly and not slouch (just like us!). To improve his walking, place some logs in his path and walk him over the logs on a short lead. The logs are the correct distance apart when your dog has to lift his feet high to step over them. If the position of the logs matches his stride, repeat this

Obstacle course at a walking pace (with treats as a reward).

several times with him. Make sure that he doesn't bounce or jump over them, though.

If you have a very small dog, you could lay out a ladder for him to climb over. Walk your dog over the

Obstacle course at a trot (with the ball as a reward).

rungs of the ladder but don't allow him to jump. This is not a race, more a balancing act.

Caution!
Argos loves his evening ritual: after the last walk, I fill his snack ball with the last of his daily rations. Before I do this, I put a resistance band (see *Useful accessories*) on the foot of the operated leg, and while he is eating his last meal, he does an extra quarter of an hour's training.

The best type of toy to fill with treats is one made of rubber, which doesn't split when the dog bites it. It's also very important to use a big enough toy so your dog can't swallow it. And the treats should be the ideal size, too; big enough so that only one falls out each time, not several all at once.

Use a portion of his usual food allowance, so that he has to work for it.

Swimming

Swimming is a perfect exercise for your dog – but only once the surgical wound has healed completely. Take advantage of lakes and streams, or wherever else dogs are allowed to swim in your area.

Do you have a paddling pool? If the weather is warm enough, and your dog is small enought to swim in it, fill it up and let him get in. Pull a toy on a string through the water, so your dog swims to catch the 'prey.' Trying to catch the toy will increase his motivation to swim.

Caution!
The floor surface of paddling pools is often too slippery for dogs. If your dog should slip, not only could this injure him, it could deter him from this exercise. Lay a non-slip mat on the floor of the paddling pool.

The treat ball keeps your dog busy and on the move, whilst the band encourages him to lift that leg higher, therefore exercising the muscle.

TIP

How about tying a ribbon or piece of exercise band around the leg which has been operated on? Some dogs will find this irritating, and will left the leg higher as they walk. Perfect! Take advantage of this response – fill a treat ball with some treats so that he's so busy trying to get these he leaves the ribbon or band alone.

Argos likes to swim, but we have only a very small pond nearby. I throw a dog chew (it floats!) into the water as far as I can. He swims out, grabs it, and then I throw another one in a different direction, and so on. On the way to getting the treat, he splashes about and gets plenty of exercise.

Caution!

Fetching or eating while swimming could cause your dog to swallow large amounts of water. Be aware that, over the next few hours, he may need to urinate more often than usual!

Does your dog love fetching, like Aisha? Then an unsinkable frisbee is perfect for him! (see *Useful accessories*). If you buy a disc, keep in mind when choosing the colour that dogs can see a light colour on a dark background, and can't distinguish between red and green. Yellow and blue are the best colours to choose.

Caution!

Throwing a stick, ball or frisbee on land is absolutely taboo, because they encourage the dog to jump up, and make sudden stops and changes of direction. If you use balls in the water then avoid tennis balls – they float and are easily visible, but are coated with a material that can be harmful to canine teeth. Make sure that the ball is sufficiently large that he doesn't get it stuck in his throat, which could cause him to choke. For a German Shepherd, a ball the size of a tennis ball could be disastrous.

Summary

We have tried our best to describe the exercises used for muscle building in clear and concise terms. The accompanying photos will enable you to see the exercises in practice, and also help you to remember each move. You can vary an exercise according to your environment.

Doing the same thing all the time isn't a good idea – and this applies to dogs just as much as humans, as Kira, Aisha, Basco, and Chico would agree. Because you will need to keep doing the same *type* of exercise, vary the actual routines day to day. Sometimes, just a different kind of reward (apple slices instead of dry food), or another toy is enough of a variation. Kira loves nothing better than a toy which grunts or squeaks, so her owner alway has a squeaky toy in her pocket in case of an emergency. If Kira seems fed up or is refusing to do any more, she can chew on the toy for a while as a reward. This will help to keep her motivated and interested in what she is doing.

Life, and certainly life with a dog, is too precious to waste doing something joyless or tedious. Find out what makes your dog tick and use this to motivate him during training. Having fun with your dog during physiotherapy and rehabilitation is most definitely possible.

We hope we have shown you how you can make training fun and varied. We wish you every success and happiness, and your dog all the best for his recovery.

Appendices

Useful accessories

Aquatherapy

You can obtain information about canine aquatherapy or hydrotherapy in the UK from the CHA (Canine Hydrotherapy Association): www.canine-hydrotherapy.org. Under the CHA Member section, you will find contact details of all approved UK canine hydrotherapy centres.

Visit www.iaamb.org for information about US-based organisations.

Bandages

This website is an online chemist for dogs! It sells almost anything you can think of, including bandages and dog socks to protect the bandages: www.bestpetpharmacy.co.uk.

Child gate/stair gate

This particular child gate comes very highly recommended. It has won several awards for its safety features and is a reasonable price, too: www.argos.co.uk/static/Product/partNumber/3763461.htm.

Classes

To find dog training classes in the UK, simply visit this website and type in your postcode or county: www.kennel-corner.co.uk.

To find out more about dog-dancing in the UK, visit this website for information and videos: www.dancingdogs.co.uk.

Clicker training

A conditioning method of dog training, a clicker, or small mechanical noisemaker, is used as a marker for behaviour. The method uses positive reinforcement because it is reward based. The clicker is used to teach a new behaviour, to enable the dog to rapidly identify that a particular behaviour is required in order to hear the noise of the clicker, and therefore receive the reward. See the following websites for more information:

www.fun4fido.co.uk has an excellent, in-depth guide to clicker training.

www.clickertrainusa.com.

www.seapets.co.uk sells clickers which come with a free guide and training tips.

There are also plenty of great clicker training videos on YouTube: www.youtube.com.

Cold/hot packs

You can buy these from any chemist and most supermarkets sell them, too. The best ones to look for are the gel packs, as these are flexible and can be wrapped around the leg, for example.

Dog ramp

Dog ramps can be very costly, but this one is a good price and comes highly recommended; visit www.bargainbrands.co.uk/dog_ramp.html.

This company makes a foldable, lightweight wooden ramp which has been recommended on several pet forums; visit www.overthetop.co.uk/shop/Tri_Fold_Car_Pet_Ramp.html.

Dog wheelchairs

www.doggon-uk.com is an excellent website which sells many types of products to help your dog stay mobile. The many customer testimonials and helpful photographs will enable you to choose the right product.

These products are also available second-hand on ebay: www.ebay.co.uk.

Food dummy/training dummy

This website offers four different varieties of training dummy, available in a choice of colours and with a sealed interior so that they will float in water: www.countrykeeper.net.

Frisbee

Available from any good toy shop.

Intelligence games for dogs/Kongs®

www.zooplus.co.uk/shop/dogs/dog_toys_dog_training/intelligence_games is a great source for all things dog-related, including accessories and intelligence games to test how clever your dog is!

Harness

www.doggiesolutions.co.uk has a large variety of harnesses to suit every dog.

Physiotherapy

www.acpat.org is the association of chartered physiotherapists in animal therapy in the UK. This website will help you find a reputable canine physiotherapist in your area.

Your vet should also be able to recommend a physiotherapist.

For US organisations/therapists, see www.caninerehabinstitute.com.

Further reading

Swim to Recovery: Canine Hydrotherapy Healing – Gentle Dog Care by Emily Wong. Published by Hubble and Hattie. ISBN: 978-1-845843-41-0.

The Complete Dog Massage Manual – Gentle Dog Care by Julia Robertson. Published by Hubble & Hattie. ISBN 978-1-845843-22-9.

Dog Relax: Relaxed Dogs, Relaxed Owners by Sabina Pilguj. Published by Hubble and Hattie. ISBN: 978-1-845843-33-5.

Exercising your Puppy: a gentle and natural approach – Gentle Dog Care by Julia Robertson and Elisabeth Pope. Published by Hubble and Hattie. ISBN: 978-1-845843-57-1.

Living with an Older Dog – Gentle Dog Care by David Alderton and Derek Hall. Published by Hubble and Hattie. ISBN: 978-1-845843-35-0.

Animal Physiotherapy: Assessment, Treatment and Rehabilitation of Animals by Catherine McGowan and Narelle Stubbs. Published by Wiley-Blackwell. ISBN: 978-1-405131-95-7.

My Dog has Hip dysplasia – but lives life to the full! by Kirsten Häusler and Barbara Friedrich. Published by Hubble and Hattie. ISBN: 978-1-845843-82-3.

My Dog is Blind – but lives life to the full! by Nicole Horsky. Published by Hubble and Hattie. ISBN: 978-1-845842-91-8.

My Dog is Deaf – but lives life to the full! by Jennifer Willms. Published by Hubble and Hattie. ISBN: 97-1-845843-81-6.

My Dog has Arthritis – but lives life to the full! by Gill Carrick. Published by Hubble and Hattie. ISBN: 978-1-845844-18-9.

Emergency First Aid for Dogs – at home and away by Martn Bucksh. Published by Hubble and Hattie. ISBN: 978-1-845843-86-1.

Gentle Dog Care

*128 pages • 100 colour photos • 20.5x20.5cm • ISBN: 978-1-845843-22-9 • £12.99**

swim to recovery
canine hydrotherapy healing

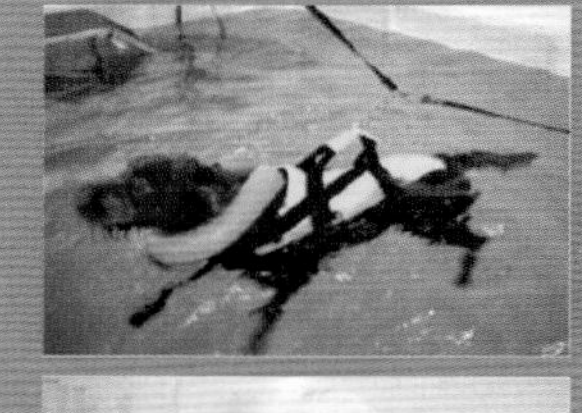

Hubble & Hattie

Emily Wong

Gentle Dog Care

*128 pages • 130+ colour photos • 20.5x20.5cm • ISBN: 978-1-845843-41-0 • £12.99**

For more info on Hubble and Hattie books, visit our website at www.hubbleandhattie.com
email info@hubbleandhattie.com • tel 44 (0)1305 260068 • *prices subject to change • p&p extra

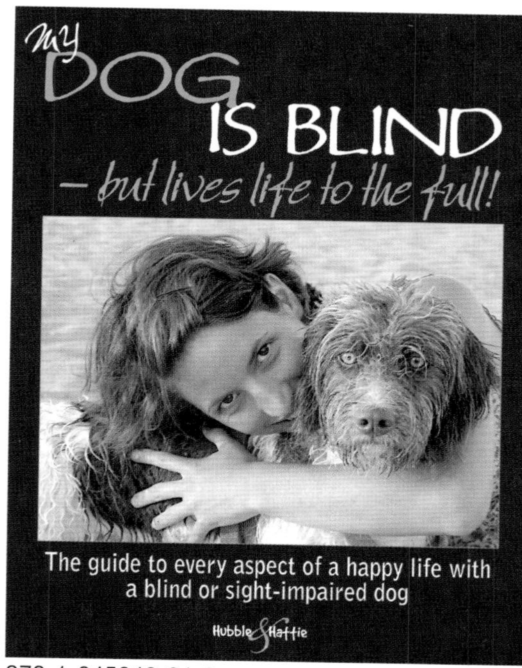

978-1-845842-91-8

978-1-845843-81-6

978-1-845843-83-0

All 80 pages • c50 colour photos • 22x17cm • £9.99* each

Index